# TO
# LIVE

TO

LIVE

# TO LIVE

**FIGHTING FOR LIFE ON THE KILLER MOUNTAIN**

## ÉLISABETH REVOL

IN COLLABORATION WITH ÉLIANE PATRIARCA
TRANSLATED BY NATALIE BERRY

Vertebrate Publishing, Sheffield
www.v-publishing.co.uk

# TO LIVE

**FIGHTING FOR LIFE ON
THE KILLER MOUNTAIN**

## ÉLISABETH
REVOL

In collaboration with Éliane Patriarca
Translated by Natalie Berry
First published in France as *Vivre* in 2019 by Arthaud (a department of Editions Flammarion, Paris).
First published in English as *To Live* in 2020 by Vertebrate Publishing.

 Vertebrate Publishing
Omega Court, 352 Cemetery Road, Sheffield S11 8FT UK.
www.v-publishing.co.uk

A CIP catalogue record for this book is available from the British Library.

ISBN: 978-1-83981-017-6 (Hardback)
ISBN: 978-1-83981-018-3 (Ebook)

10 9 8 7 6 5 4 3 2 1

 Cover design by Jane Beagley, Vertebrate Publishing.
Production by Cameron Bonser, Vertebrate Publishing.
www.v-publishing.co.uk

Vertebrate Publishing is committed to printing on paper from sustainable sources.

Printed and bound in the UK by T.J. International Ltd, Padstow, Cornwall.

# CONTENTS

---

# 23 MAY 2019,
# 10.50 A.M.

The summit of Everest! The view is exceptional, as are the emotions that are surging through me. Such beauty! What a divine gift to be here, high on the highest mountain on Earth, among these icy sentries. I have finally realised my childhood dream; I have a new lease of life, I am reborn.

Since my return from Nanga Parbat in February 2018, this has been the project I have clung on to. Everest is what has 'taken hold' of me, kept me alive, despite the black chasms of despair into which I have so often sunk.

I had finally gone back home to the Drôme. After two days in an Islamabad hospital, I had arrived in France on 30 January 2018. I then spent an exhausting week of intensive care in hospital in Sallanches, where I was stormed by the media. That was followed by a press conference in Chamonix on 7 February, as I was just coming to realise – or rather admit – that there was no longer any hope of saving my climbing partner Tomek; where, despite being exhausted and in shock, I had tried to answer questions.[1] Doctors had requested a further assessment of my frostbite in six weeks' time.

During this 'recovery' period, one of my sponsors, the founder of TeamWork Voile et Montagne, Philippe Rey-Gorrez, visited me. He asked me which projects remained close to my heart. As a girl, I told him, I had dreamt each night beneath a poster of Everest.

This mountain was my first dream, the root of my passion. In May 2017, I had spent two perfect months in the Himalaya, wandering among the giants of our planet – visiting Makalu, summiting Lhotse and then confronting Everest, alone, without oxygen. My heart fluttered with the euphoria and joy of finally treading on the flanks of this mountain! But at around 8,400 or 8,500 metres, a blizzard and extremely cold temperatures convinced me to give up. Returning to Everest would be financially challenging; my dream would remain unfulfilled. 'The day you decide to go back to Everest,' Philippe Rey-Gorrez told me straight, 'I'll be there to help you. You can explore the mountain without oxygen, but with backup: someone to follow you with oxygen in case you have a problem.' A rush of warmth ran through me, a burst of life that softened my heart, which until this point had been hardened like a stone. Hearing these words, I imagined myself at the Icefall in an instant. I saw my bivouac at Camp 4 under the twinkling stars and the beautiful full moon. I imagined myself on the Hillary Step, breathless and slow, but brimming with emotion. Our meeting was brief and informal, but this project lit up the depths of my despair and, for the first time since my return to France, I glimpsed a ray of light …

It was this idea that brought me back to life; I thought about it all year. I discussed it immediately with Jean-Christophe, my husband, and with Ludovic Giambiasi, my best friend and personal 'route planner'. I told them that the one last project close to my heart in my life as a Himalayan mountaineer was Everest. I thought about it each time I found myself spiralling downwards, drowning in a hell of guilt and bitter memories.

One year later, in April 2019, I left for the high mountains again, heading for the Baltoro glacier in Pakistan, the land of thin air that has held a magnetic attraction for me since I first discovered it in 2008. As I packed my bag, I was rattled by contradictory emotions: joy, a feeling of freedom, a sense of taking revenge on the previous year, a conviction that it was now or never. But also plenty of nerves and fear, relating to me: my capacity to bear the cold in my fragile extremities, my capacity to return to the high mountains, to go back to high-altitude bivouacs, with my memories of people dear to me who had touched my life and left too soon.

I am *addicted* to the mountains. I have been acutely aware of this since my return from Nanga. Previously, on my return from Annapurna in 2009, I had gone through a dreadful phase of questioning, of doubt. When you are defeated, you interrogate yourself about the irresistible attraction that constantly draws you up there. You also come to understand that you're caught in a trap.

I was twenty years old when I caught the climbing bug. I binged on summits. I ascended many routes and faces in the Alps over a period of ten years. I was looking for difficulty and performance. Effort, elevation, excitement, stress, questions, then fulfilment – this cocktail satisfied me a little more each time. When I discovered the Himalaya in 2007, an infinite universe of exploration opened up to me: discovering new summits, but also testing my aptitudes and my limits in the troposphere.

Even though I have lived through some terribly difficult, unbearable things in the high mountains, my attraction to them remains strong. It's difficult to explain, just as it is to understand. But it's an environment I can't do without; or, rather, one which I couldn't do without for more than a decade.

Now, with this Everest expedition, I might succeed in ending this chapter of my life, closing the loop and leaving behind the passion that has made me live intensely, but which is also devouring, limiting and obsessive, and which sometimes gets the better of me.

I had initially considered a return to the Diamir Valley, to Nanga Parbat. For Tomek, to calm my memories. But after the deaths of Daniele Nardi and Tom Ballard last March on the slopes of this mountain, I know that I won't go back there. The loss left me devastated and stalled my thoughts. Nanga had caught hold of me again. Daniele was a very close friend and he had contributed to my and Tomek's

3

rescue. One year later, I found myself 'on the other side', liaising day and night with the rescue team in Pakistan, who I was trying to help given my familiarity with the route up the Mummery Spur. I was waiting, powerless, behind the screen and on the telephone, just as Daniele had been when he came to my aid in 2018. In vain.

Through this tragedy, I relived and better understood what had happened with Tomek and me on Nanga in 2018, after the summit: the interest stirred up by drama in the mountains, from the media and in part from the 'audience', via the 'live show' offered by social media. The gap between what one lives and suffers up there and the instantaneous interpretations; the analysts who each give their version, their view; the insults and defamations which fly around on social networks, plunging the family into a twofold chaos; and the rumours, too, which form the basis of hateful judgements. But who knows the exact circumstances? Who was actually there?

This new drama didn't put paid to my dream of Everest, however. The project is very far removed from my usual climbing style, but this year I've put this aside – with good reason. I've abandoned my Himalayan approach of discovering the unknown. I've also let go of any idea of performance. What I have come to look for on Everest this time is very different, intimate, personal. A normal route, that's fine by me; I don't want to take risks. Above all, I no longer want to impose that on Jean-Christophe. Maybe I pushed my commitment too far: the accident and Tomek's death were harsh reminders of life's fragility.

I left for Everest feeling calm, because my quest was different. It would be impossible for me today to set off in a roped team on an exposed route, impossible above all to take responsibility for someone else again in the Himalaya.

I also feel lighter in spirit, because I have finally written *our* account of Nanga Parbat. I have recounted our journey with my words, our convictions, our fight; and laid out the facts that don't appear in the news reports, those which form the reality of our ascent. I owed it to Tomek.

# 25 JANUARY 2018,
# NANGA PARBAT (PAKISTAN), CAMP 4

At dawn, the top of the Mazeno Ridge is already gleaming in the skimming light of the low sun, a light that rises from the abyss. The landscape opens up; the sky passes from grey to blue. The day promises to be beautiful. Finally! For three weeks, we have been trapped by bad weather in Kutgali, at 3,800 metres. The jet stream has dominated Nanga and never dropped below seventy to eighty kilometres per hour at 6,500 metres. Above, it has been stormy with winds reaching up to 150 kilometres per hour. Today, finally, we are leaving for the summit of Nanga Parbat!

We move forward, one behind the other. Slow, steady. I appreciate this time. I don't need to concentrate; I switch to autopilot mode and I can clear my head of thoughts.

It's forty-five days since we landed in Islamabad, one month since we arrived in the Himalaya at the foot of the ninth-highest summit in the world at 8,125 metres. Its name means 'Naked Mountain'. It is sometimes called Diamir or 'King of Mountains'; or even 'Killer Mountain', as more than thirty mountaineers died on its slopes before the Austrian Hermann Buhl managed to reach the summit in 1953.

This is Tomek's seventh attempt to summit Nanga Parbat, my fourth, and our third attempt together: in winter 2015 we had ascended to 7,800 metres, in 2016 to 7,500 metres. But bad weather had chased us away twice.

Shortly before 6 a.m., I sent a message to my husband, Jean-Christophe, from Camp 4. I left my satellite phone, the Thuraya, at Base Camp, because we don't have a generator to charge it, contrary to what was agreed with Ali, our agent. So I'm using the 'message' function of the inReach, my GPS tracker. Exchanges are cryptic: 160 characters maximum, typed letter by letter:

*Yes we feel ok we try something today if weather ok if not we descend.*[2]

We also exchanged weather information with my good friend Ludovic, who is controlling the logistics of our expedition from his home in Gap in south-eastern France; and with Anna, Tomek's wife.

Tomek and I didn't set off until 7.30 a.m. We were slow to get started because he couldn't warm up his feet. It was crucial to address this before leaving. We used the stove to thaw the liner, the inner shell and the outer boot. While he was putting on one boot, I was warming the other foot. It was time-consuming and ineffective. Due to sweating and excessively cold temperatures, it's difficult to keep our shoes dry: they freeze on the inside and the outside. Even when walking, it's impossible to warm them up. Tom paid a high price in 2015 on Nanga with his frostbitten feet. So our motto this year is to protect and insulate the boots against humidity. We're storing our liners in our sleeping bags to dry them out overnight and to keep them at a higher temperature. In Islamabad, we also considered wrapping our feet in a sheet of aluminium foil to insulate them from 5,800 metres and above, a method that we are testing today. I have deviated from one of my rules: 'Don't experiment on summit day.' And I've been regretting this since leaving our crevasse bivouac. The aluminium foil seems to be freezing my toes instead of insulating them. Too bad – we've already left; we'll continue. If I get too cold, I'll remove it later. Tom isn't complaining – it must be working for him.

We have left all our gear at Camp 4 – at an altitude of 7,300 metres – inside the crevasse where we bivvied. We have to make the journey to and from the summit within the day. This is the most enjoyable stage of an ascent: no need to carry a rucksack any more, no more camps to move. We are carrying just one litre of water each, three cereal bars, our goggles, our GoPros and cameras, an altitude pharmacy for two, my inReach, a pair of gloves and an emergency pair of mitts.

We savour the lightness of the air, of our bodies, the renewed nimbleness of our movements, but with a contradicting sensation: without a rucksack we're flying, but the altitude is weighing us down.

We don't speak; each of us economises our breath. Only our breathing, our movements and a light wind whistling around our ears breaks the silence through the down hood and the many layers stacked underneath: balaclava, hat, polar jacket with hood, lightweight down jacket. From time to time, an odd word to keep in contact:

'Are you OK, Tom?'

'Yes, I'm OK, Éli.'

'OK, perfect!'

Up here, long sentences don't work any more. We had discussed our communication codes and safety protocols at length beforehand. We both know that we're alone, with neither help nor rescue possible beyond our own means. We have talked about this together so often.

We cross a huge crevasse. My internal metronome is triggered and I pick up my pace, move faster; I go for it. It's our routine in the mountains. Tom is like a tractor, a diesel engine; whereas I'm more like a gutsy petrol engine, fast. I can get going quickly in the morning without warming up; he likes to walk alone, to speak to Fairy, the goddess of Nanga Parbat, and his rate of ascent is slow. I also like to climb alone, sometimes by the light of my head torch or the moon, sometimes under the comforting daytime sun; and to give free rein to the emotions I keep to myself when we're together. This is time in which I allow myself to dream, to think ahead, to marvel in this cirque of ice, in the wonderful crisp air above the snowy vastness.

Tomek and I are proud to once again be attempting this mountain in pure alpine style.[3] To ascend and descend very quickly and emerge unscathed in this universe of rarefied air where our capabilities are diminished. Without leaving traces of our passage, without external help or oxygen, in keeping with our ethics and our philosophy in the mountains. Over the course of our expeditions here, we have acquired a very specific knowledge of Nanga and of our aptitude at these altitudes. On an ascent of this kind, you must be bonded, complement each other. Tomek and I embody this. Always quick to remotivate the other. We decide on everything together; our roped team functions simply, frankly and in an uncomplicated manner. If one of us feels unwell, we turn around without regret or guilt.

The weather conditions are harsh here, especially this winter, which is colder than ever. There is no room for error, we're conscious of this. But we often tell ourselves: 'A difficult day up here is always easier than a day's work down there!' It's tough, but we love this aspect. Maybe it's in the effort, in surpassing ourselves, that we find satisfaction. To manage your body, to try not to listen to the first signs of pain, to keep going, not give up and ignore the little voice inside which sometimes asks: 'But what the hell are you doing here? There's no point; stop!'

We are now below the summit pyramid. Immense. We continue traversing along the bottom of the face. The terrain is more inclined and there are breaks in the glacier. We bypass several crevasses. From a distance, the glaciers always appear flat and the going looks easy. In amongst them, it's often a real disaster zone. Fortunately, it hasn't snowed much this winter and the wind has swept all the snowfall away. The crevasses are very open and visible.

An old fixed rope hangs down. A remnant that has survived the melting of the glacier? The mountain has been different since yesterday. Until then, we were progressing in virgin terrain. From this point on, the terrain bears the traces of a multitude of expeditions that have passed by over so many years. Yesterday, we glimpsed a tent at Camp 4 of the normal route, below our own camp. Today, there are fixed ropes and the remains of tents. Reassuring traces, but also confusing.

A few steps further on, there are more fixed ropes, much more recent, of the type that high-altitude Sherpas place in order to facilitate and secure the flow of their clients, installed on the traverse that we have to take. 'Have you seen the fixed ropes, Tom? Strange that they're still there after autumn, isn't it?' Generally in winter they're covered by snow and trapped in the ice.

I follow the ropes, then bear right until I reach a rocky island in the middle of the slope. The void opens up under my feet as the slope tilts and straightens. It's vast. Where to go now? Fortunately, beyond the island, the ropes continue and indicate the route. I don't use the fixed ropes; I have no confidence in them. So I dig in my crampons and my axes to traverse the icy section. The ice is hard. I have to readjust my picks twice, dislodging one or two bombs of icy plates. A sign of bad ice. I regain my footing in the snow. I glance at Tom. He's not very far away. I'll wait for him in the sun; it's too cold here! The traverse is very long and several kilometres in ascent; the remaining metres to the summit will be hard-won in this terrain.

## 10.45 A.M. ALTITUDE: 7,500 METRES +

Finally, I reach the sunshine. I can make the most of its divine warmth. I sit down and sacrifice a cereal bar in celebration. The setting is magnificent. My face is covered in frost. My jaw is stiff, cemented by the morning cold and icy breeze.

Tom arrives. He's doing well and looking good with his frosted beard. We feel good. The sky veils slightly while the temperature continues to drop, so I start walking again. But after a few metres, I realise that under this very deceptive cloudy veil, the UV radiation is extremely high. I open my rucksack and pull out my goggles. I turn around:

'Tom, are you putting your goggles on? Be careful of the sun!'

'Yes, Éli, don't worry!'

I continue at my own pace; Tomek follows some tens of metres behind. We are two solitary people on this huge mountain, but we are not afraid of it – quite the contrary. We love it, this limitless freedom! We came in search of it.

I ascend in the direction of a snowy arête and a small vertical col to the right of the summit. I want to set foot on it. Tom shouts that I need to head left, that the summit is on the axis. I know, Tom; I just want to see what's beyond. A rocky summit in the distance intrigues me. I want to measure the immense scale and grandeur of this place. At the col, I continue a bit beyond to look. I've had this wretched compulsion from a young age: to see what lies above or behind, whether the view is different! I let my eyes take it all in. In the depths of the sky, the Mazeno Ridge shears through the backdrop. Small shimmering particles line the sky, creating a ballet of light. The wind whistles and sweeps clouds of snow into the distance. I see this but I don't hear it, being bundled up and insulated in my hats, hoods and multiple jackets. For a moment, I immerse myself in this beauty.

We're lucky to have been completely sheltered since the sun kissed the face. I retrace my steps and pause while waiting for Tom. I drink; I eat a cereal bar.

We are more than 7,500 metres above sea level. For mountaineers, it's a symbolic threshold, entering what is called 'the Death Zone'. I don't like this term much, nor the notion, but nonetheless I pay attention to it today. Our acclimatisation is far from optimal, as the bad weather disrupted our schedule. I am well; I know the limits of where my body can go. But I stay alert to any messages it might send me. Now I'm hungry – that's a good sign!

I have the topo in my head, and I've been refreshing my memory repeatedly since Base Camp: 'Follow the ramp which ascends diagonally right to a small col; then trend diagonally left until the start of the flared couloir; then go up the rightwards-trending couloir directly above; then traverse right before the couloir's exit, between the main summit and the north summit; and finally ascend a mixed section trending diagonally right to the summit.'

But in the depths of this field of snow and ice, everything is less clear. I must concentrate to discern, study, cross-check, decide.

Dimensions change, landmarks disappear. It's easy enough to get lost on a route in the Alps, despite the very detailed topos and logical lines of ascent. Here, it's a kingdom of excess: walls without end; fields of sharpened ice, filed and polished over the years by the snow and wind; mixed and rocky plateaus ...

In the middle of the pyramid, we enter a mixed zone directly below the summit. We have to weave between the snowy ramps, looking for the line of weakness.[4] Looking, navigating, ascending, descending, climbing, downclimbing, traversing while balanced on the front points of our crampons. Grasping rocky edges with the tips of our fingers in gloved hands. Ensuring sufficient grip to safely 'walk the tightrope'. The scale disconcerts me: it's far from what I had imagined. Tom and I exchange looks regularly; we communicate at a distance. I need to share my doubts about our route with him. He is always trusting; he agrees with me and follows me.

My concentration is such that I don't pay attention to anything else. I limit my field of vision to a radius of fifty metres: either towards the top of the face, or behind me to check that Tom is still following. The rock is compact. A mix of granite, gneiss and pegmatite. My crampons grip the rocky edges; the terrain becomes more sustained and the difficulties gradually increase as we ascend. I clear holds covered in snow. The wind is still dormant, thank God. When I turn to look at Tom and assure myself that everything is OK, my eyes fall on the Mazeno Ridge to the right – it's blowing over there.

I like these sections where I'm very focused, in a perfect state of calm. Concentrating on the precision of my steps, the grip of my hands, I can propel myself on to the next holds. Time fades. The air is getting thinner. My heart beats faster; I gasp with each step. Everything here is of staggering scale.

We have been moving without a rope since this morning; we left it at Camp 4. Tomek and I felt that we wouldn't need it.

We speak very little.

'Are you OK?'

'Yes.'

'OK.'

We move forward, each of us concentrated in our bubble. The further I go, the more the distance between us widens.

Tomek really doesn't like this terrain. 'Éli! Should we escape left in the couloir?'

He's right: we're not very fast and we're losing time in this mixed ground. 'Let's go!'

There's a line of weakness level with me. I wait for Tomek at the edge of the couloir, which is streaked with waves of hard snow sculpted by swirls of wind. I have only seen this once before in the mountains, under the east summit of Annapurna in 2009: waves over a metre high spanning the numerous kilometres of the arête, and hundreds of powder plumes falling into white dust on the south face. It was a striking spectacle. Tomek joins me. In the meantime, I have scoped out the rest of the route.

The effort is monotonous: plant an axe, place a pole, left crampon then right crampon. I hardly ever take a break, whereas Tom stops and starts repeatedly. Thirty or forty steps and he allows himself a pause to breathe: thirty seconds or a minute of rest. Then off again.

> Upon my return, I will learn that at this moment in time Altaf, a Pakistani soldier at Base Camp, is watching us. He sees us and sends a message to Ali Saltoro, our agent. 'They are above 8,000 metres. They are ascending, moving forwards.' Ali passes this message on to Ludo in France, and to my mountaineer friend Daniele Nardi in Italy. The information diffuses rapidly on the internet. But a sea of clouds coming from the Rupal Face floods the Mazeno Ridge and reaches the Diamir Valley. No more visibility for us or them. From that point, we are isolated in these upper spheres.

The couloir straightens up a bit and the wind-sculpted waves in the ice become even more imposing.

The temperature is mild; I feel good.

My eyes wander and my gaze falls on two cairns on the arête: two heaps of stones that attract my attention, distracting me. I turn to see where Tomek is.

The sun starts to sink lower. The sky loses its azure colour and turns yellow. It must be late. The sun lights up Nanga, the only summit to emerge from the clouds. Wind blows on the Mazeno Ridge. Clouds scatter and surround the pyramid above its base. The landscape is magical. We're not far from the last summit triangle. But what time is it? I switch on the inReach to check the altitude and time, and find two messages: one from my husband, the other from Ludo. But typing is far too laborious at this altitude. I was scarcely able to take off my gloves to switch it on without my hands starting to hurt. I only share my position to reassure them: 8,036 metres, 5.15 p.m. Not too bad altitude-wise, but a bit late timing-wise … We lost time in the mixed zone below, meandering too much, for sure. And Camp 4 was a long way from the summit this morning. But we had no choice yesterday: it was a white-out and we were bathed in sleet, with no visibility, so it was impossible to reach the foot of the pyramid.

We are ninety metres from the summit after ten hours of walking. I switch off the inReach and put it back in my down jacket to save the battery. Even if it means freezing fingers, I want to quickly immortalise this incredible atmosphere! I get the GoPro out and, while filming, reflect on where to go from here. I place my trust in my camera. During my expeditions, it has become a confidante that helps me to overcome loneliness. I see Tomek advancing at his own pace; he's fine. I'm happy that he's on his feet today. He's been suffering from digestive problems since mid-January. Hygiene at Base Camp left a lot to be desired for our 'sanitised' stomachs: the cooking was done on a clay floor, and our chef, Sharkan, had rather grubby hands for kneading the dough and making *chapatis*, cutting the meat and lighting the fire. The water was sometimes barely boiled. Tomek, despite his ultra-hardy nature, was affected by this lack of hygiene for the first time.

In bad shape, he obsessed over this problem throughout our days there: he was curiously persuaded that the origin of his digestive troubles lay in the bread cooked by Sharkan, who had been 'tasked' with causing his summit attempt to fail! I hadn't seen Tomek in this state of mind – embittered, sour – since Simone Moro ravaged *his* mountain by achieving the first winter ascent of Nanga Parbat in February 2016. Resentful to the point of paranoia. I feel as though he's changed a lot; he seems depressed, too. At Base Camp, I suffered from this heavy atmosphere, desperate to bring Tomek back to reason, to reality.

Fortunately, since our arrival at Camp 2 at 6,600 metres, and after the rest day on 22 January, he seems to have recovered. He's eating better, smiling and singing once again.

I hear the crunching of his crampons. I call out to him.

'Tom, how are you feeling?'

'Good, OK. You?'

'Great. Tom, what shall we do? It's 5.15 p.m. and we're at 8,036 metres. The Mazeno Ridge is covered with cloud. We won't be able to see anything. What do you want to do? Should we continue or descend? It'll be tough and we'll arrive in the dark if we continue.'

'Let's continue. We're not very far away. It's not too cold.'

If one of us had shown the slightest hesitation or put forward an argument against our pursuit of the summit, we would have descended immediately. But both of us remained in the dynamic of ascent, without delving too deep into our decision.

Tomek is motivated; I am too. I'm worried about the late time, about the darkness that's due to fall – Tomek too, certainly – but desire and emotion prevail. I am armed with my experience of a night descent after summiting Lhotse (8,516 metres), Everest's high neighbour, last May. I remember immense joy and warmer temperatures in the evening than at the start of the day. I tell myself that the cold is bearable, manageable. The clouds will block our view, of course, but we can continue. We are here to try our best.

I have interrogated myself a lot about the decisions we took throughout this day. In the mountains, I'm constantly making decisions, quickly analysing and making a choice. But there, ninety metres from the summit of Nanga Parbat, another factor came into play: the expectant emotion of reaching the summit, the *feeling*, its effect on me, the pleasure and the value that I attribute to this ascent. At that moment, I think Tom was experiencing the same emotion, and we quickly decided together to continue.

We climb the couloir in the same monotonous motion as before. It's a long climb. The route continues endlessly; the summit has not yet been revealed. Intense, magical. I watch the mist that covers the whole valley, fearing that it will envelop us both at once and isolate us from each other. But the threatening mantle seems to be settled below.

The shadows stretch and lengthen. The sun will set soon. In a moment, the cold will be intense and bitter, but the sunset is dazzling. In my life as a Himalayan mountaineer, I have never seen such a beautiful spectacle. Magical. The sea of cotton-like clouds covers all the mountains except for Nanga, which tears majestically through the purple sky. Here we are, the sky passing from pink to a bright and cold shade of blue, from a warm atmosphere to a biting cold.

My crampons anchor in the hard, wind-blown snow. A few metres above, the couloir exit comes into view. Go slowly and don't think, almost on autopilot.

The terrain becomes drier, more mixed. We are to the left of the summit. We traverse, ascending rightwards. Darkness falls. I pull out my head torch. I wait for Tomek. The detail of the terrain is erased by the half-light. My visual field is reduced to the beam of my torch, focused on the twenty metres ahead of me. Tomek's face is covered with icy flakes. We manage to articulate a few words, despite our stiffened jaws:

'Are you OK?'

'Yes.'

'Do you feel good? Yes? Not too cold?'

'It hurts, but it's bearable!'

'Should we continue?'

'Yes!'

Each metre travelled is a small victory; each additional step is progress. Short of breath, we ascend together towards the starry sky.

In this moment, I realise that we will reach the summit. For me, this is the culmination of more than a decade of dreams, fantasies and questions. I flew over Nanga Parbat in August 2008 when I was returning to Islamabad from Skardu after my first experience of the 8,000-metre peaks on the Baltoro. An imposing and perfect mass of ice, with magnificent lines and serrated arêtes. My heart immediately fell for this impressive mountain; my gaze was drawn to its expanse of snow and rock.

Climbing this summit in winter? Unachievable, impossible, I said to myself back then, when the world of 8,000-metre peaks in winter seemed inaccessible to me. But this realm of questions and the unknown piqued my curiosity. Five years later, I felt ready to confront the challenges of this Himalayan giant, in my eyes one of the most aesthetic high peaks and a mountain steeped in history. I had an exciting and ambitious objective: to succeed in making the first winter ascent of Nanga Parbat in alpine style.

The Himalaya in winter fascinate me. For me, this is extreme adventure, the pinnacle of what can be achieved in the mountains. Following one of my returns from Nanga, I wrote: 'On this mountain, every day is a reward, a step towards the unknown, a step towards the discovery of oneself and one's potential. We seized these moments up there, where the heart is self-sufficient, filled with joie de vivre.' These places take me back to the wonder of childhood, to those very early days when one discovers the world.

So in January 2013, I left for Nanga Parbat with Daniele Nardi and a tight budget, as always! After so many years spent dreaming of this mountain in winter, it was magical to set foot on its slopes. At almost every step, I was moved by what I was seeing and feeling. We attempted an alpine-style ascent via the Mummery Spur on two occasions, a few days apart. A route which had never been climbed in summer, let alone in winter! A changing weather forecast, a tempestuous wind and snow got the better of us. But I had discovered the winter solitude of the Himalaya, the unspoilt coolness where the pace of life slows down and flows silently. A universe petrified by the cold, swept by fierce winds. I had returned enchanted, fascinated by the Himalaya in winter, permanently captivated by this pearl of a mountain!

In 2015, I returned with Tomek. We followed the 2000 Messner route, climbing in alpine style without fixed ropes, Sherpas or supplementary oxygen. As the only people in the world above 6,000 metres for four or five days, in an atmosphere of exceptional cold, we fought against the elements to our limits. But the changing weather forced us to turn around at 7,800 metres. The following year, we were back. But this time, we ran into lots of expedition teams at Base Camp, all attracted by the desire to make the first winter ascent. I didn't like the atmosphere – nobody was speaking openly and we were all watching each other. On 23 January, Tomek and I reached 7,500 metres, but the extreme cold (-50° Celsius) forced us to turn back and not commit to an exposed ascent, partly due to the nature of the route, but also because of the temperatures and the approaching jet stream. Continuing would perhaps have meant passing the point of no return.

For his part, Tomek has already made six attempts to tackle Nanga in winter and to come close to the goddess who fascinates him so much: Fairy.

Today, we are finally going to reach this long-coveted summit together! My heart is racing. The emotion is immense, overwhelms me. I want to shout with joy, but the cold freezes my voice. I want to cry, but my tears freeze instantly.

These are the final metres. I get the sense that the beam of Tom's head torch behind me is fading into the distance.

The night thickens between us. But I keep an eye on his light, which is getting smaller. I arrive at the little col. Polar gusts rush into my neck, pierce my bones, whip my face and snatch handfuls of ice fragments from the hard snow and throw them at me. These icy filings sting my face, slicing into my narrowed eyes. I have never experienced such cold. I get a move on; I can't hang around here. I readjust the position of my chin under the collar of my suit. I fasten my hood. Each metre is a new victory over myself. I breathe in and breathe out rapidly to go faster, but the altitude quickly suffocates me. My muscles instantly contract. I move forward in Robocop mode; I race to the top.

It must be 6 p.m. Or maybe 6.30 p.m.? Or later, I don't know. Breathless, I traverse the final metres to reach a pile of stones from which a stake entwined with fixed ropes emerges. The summit!

I fall to my knees facing the stake, turning my back to the wind to protect myself from the icy gusts. I slap my arms, my thighs, my calves, I try to warm myself up. I gasp. The wind draws glistening trails of snow in the air. I calm down, I breathe deeply. I am between two worlds: the earth and the sky. My knees are fully glued to the ground by gravity, but my hands are touching the heavens.

The wholeness of the place intoxicates me. After battling through this long day, I finally emerge among the stars.

I wait for Tomek; I watch the light of his head torch draw nearer. He is very close. I shiver with the cold, which is brutal and extreme. It's as though I'm anaesthetised. Numbed by all the years of dreaming, by the intense cold, I struggle to unravel dream from reality. Only my fight to warm up confirms to me that the situation is very real, no longer a fantasy. In the halo of my head torch, the prayer flags, frosted, mummified by the winter, are still dancing in the wind.

I'm on the summit of Nanga in winter, ten years after falling in love with this mountain. I don't take out my inReach or my GoPro, because that would mean taking off my gloves and I don't want to. I can't. I'm chilled, frozen. I want to stay here until Tomek arrives, to celebrate and to hold him in my arms. We finally have our Nanga! We have been trembling with desire for it for years; we wanted to get here so badly! This day has been so long and so difficult!

As always, when I arrive at the summit, I don't think of anything for a few minutes; I simply soak in these unique places. During an ascent, I experience irrepressible surges of joy and avalanches of emotions, my heart pounds, I shout and cry with delight; on the summit, on the other hand, I never let myself become overwhelmed by emotion. Is it a form of self-control to keep my feet on the ground, a rule that I impose subconsciously, given that I know you haven't really reached the summit until you get back down? You savour the taste of the summit on the return to Base Camp, with the risk mitigated and adrenaline levels diminished. It's always like this.

Now I think about the descent, which will require even more commitment. The loop will only be closed upon arrival at Camp 4 this evening, then at Base Camp tomorrow. We can only talk about the summit there, not before then.

# 25 JANUARY 2018,
## SUMMIT OF NANGA PARBAT,
## ALTITUDE: 8,125 METRES

---

I wait for Tomek to get here to capture this moment and, most importantly, to hug him tight. We have achieved our dream, after so many years spent piecing this ascent together. It's the most beautiful thing that we have experienced. His pace is slow but steady; his face is masked by the light from his head torch. Frosty crystals reflect in relief on his right cheek. He must be numb with cold and fatigue. I sit up on my legs to hug him. His blue eyes, now very close to me, are painted with crystals. Our happiness can explode now that we're both together at the top! I shout: 'Tomek! Yessssss!'

'Éli, what's happening with my eyes? Éli, I can't see your head torch any more; you're a blur!'

This second lasts an eternity. Everything changes. I retch and shake; fear overwhelms me. My legs turn to jelly and I collapse. Tomek's words ricochet in my head. I want them to go away, for them not to exist. I don't want to hear the unbearable, the irremediable. But his frightened eyes under his frosted eyelashes anchor his words in my heart and in my head.

From the fabulous dream in which I was soaring, I fall into a black abyss. It's not possible. It's a nightmare; I'm going to wake up! It's just my brain not working properly! But my body is trembling, I'm shivering, I'm overwhelmed by panic. My brain makes shortcuts based on situations I've lived through previously in the mountains.

It flits from hope to despair in the fraction of a second. From illusion to disillusionment. Tomek is blind on the summit of his Holy Grail! I shut my eyelids tight; my tears freeze instantly, petrified. I can no longer see. I rub my eyes. The crystals scratch like sandpaper.

Today, what hurts me most when I think back to this moment is that Tomek wasn't able to see this summit he wanted so much. It was as though this Grail was forbidden to him …

We are at 8,125 metres, completely alone, and Tomek can't see any more! What if I'm unable to help him? What if I can't get him down? In the dark, the bitter cold and the extreme altitude! I am devastated. In a fraction of a second, everything has changed dramatically; we have entered 'survival' mode. But what are we both still doing here? We have to descend. I have to react quickly. I force myself to control my anxiety. I have to concentrate and detach emotionally. I have to be pragmatic. I have to manage this difficulty. Like in 2015 when Tomek had plunged into a crevasse, shouting 'Éli! Éeeelliii! Éeeelllllliiii!', which echoed as he fell. I think I can still hear him. But today we are at the summit, at more than 8,000 metres, with Base Camp at 4,200 metres and, before that, a rising traverse above Camp 4: a 'trap' on the route that we had chosen in case of a problem.

I approach Tom and hug him. We huddle together. Time freezes for a moment. Reason comes back to me: we have to act fast, descend quickly. I have to be Tom's eyes, his guide. 'Don't worry, Tom. Hold my shoulder and we'll go down.' I keep my right arm wrapped around his shoulder, make him pivot around himself and accompany him into the wind.

While giving him these words of encouragement, I drown in dread. I can delude myself no longer; this is a catastrophe and it's up to me to manage it. We both have to make it out alive. Fleeing to the bottom is our only hope. We will take our time, but we will survive.

I take his left hand and place it on my right shoulder.

'Hold yourself there, Tom; hold on to me. Keep your hand on my shoulder. Don't let go. We'll go slowly. Don't worry – it'll be fine.'

'Yes, Éli.'

His voice doesn't sound good. He's scared. I feel as though he's a lost child. His blind eyes reflect such distress!

I move forward, my heart pounding, my mind overwhelmed. The terrain in the first metres is relatively easy. I'm pushed to my limits. The cold pierces my bones. I squint in the face of the incessant, icy, brutal wind. Tears freeze instantly on my lashes and on my cheek. I wipe my eyes with my glove; I can no longer see. 'Are you OK, Tom?' I turn around. His face seems petrified, marbled in blue and white. Covered in crystals. Everything is frosted: his eyes, the little patches of red downy hair on his cheeks. 'Yes, Éli. I'm cold. But I'm fine.' My anxiety subsides a little, and we find a rhythm. Slow, very slow; but we descend, and each step is a victory towards life, towards Base Camp.

In this mixed terrain of snow, ice and rock, I have to place each crampon point with meticulous care. All my energy is focused on the precision of my steps, Tom's steps and the pendulum motion between us. I don't think about what comes next. I'm in the present moment. My first step down is taken slowly, so as to keep Tomek in balance on my shoulder. Each step demands such concentration that I forget about the cold. Breathing suspended, muscles tensed, stomach knotted, I sense Tomek's slightest movement with tenfold precision. We are one now. I have become his eyes, my legs are his legs, my arms are his arms, and my voice guides us. I'm afraid of the cold – I'm already frozen and in the inherent slowness of the situation, I don't know how long I'll last.

Tomek is still resting on my shoulder. I alternate between left and right, following the slope of the terrain. I have to find appropriate, effective moves and repeat them. Repetition of movement is something I've practised since childhood. I was a gymnast until the age of eighteen, and was educated, trained and conditioned in rehearsing sequences to achieve efficient motion. So this logical construction of moves, as regulated as possible, comes automatically. I place one foot and then the other. I lean on an axe; the other is clipped to my gear loop. Then I repeat the same thing for Tomek, and I control his steps and his body position as though they were mine. And so on. A routine is established, helping me to forget everything else for the space of a second. I'm cold, and so is Tomek. I know that we're making slow progress, but we're descending.

A whirlwind of questions assails me again: will I succeed in getting Tomek down in this rugged terrain? How long will it take? Numb with cold, we won't last long. My objective is to reach Camp 4. I have to split up the route, step by step. I set myself a goal, a point to reach. Then the next one, once the first has been reached. The mixed ground first of all. The couloir next. After that, we'll see. I accept the idea that it'll be a long, appalling night. The cold? The wind? Moving is our only way out. Don't stop, get down, keep moving about to maintain our circulation, and head forwards in the depths of this night, vanishing into the darkness in front of us. I have to fight for him, for both of us, and get him down!

I'm very cold. Sometimes, I have to pause to focus on keeping my whole body going: make big circles with my arms, jump on the spot, slap my knees to get as much blood as possible to my extremities. Rub Tomek's back. Make him move as much as possible while he seems frozen, mummified. Encourage him.

My head torch lights up only what lies right in front of me. I know there's a void and a slope around it, but I force myself to focus on this halo and the present moment. Our survival depends on it. Make my steps. Then Tom's. Our two bodies in balance. Concentrating on the present moment, on the technical steps, clears my questions and fears for a short while; I'm just obsessed with the sequence of movements to complete. The movements of crampons—contact—shoulder link together in an almost automatic rhythm.

Time fades, warps. I talk to Tomek as much as I can and as much as the terrain allows me to. I motivate him; I try to give him hope. I talk to him about his life in Ireland, his children, Anna, the summit, and about the warmth that we'll savour once we return to Base Camp. But he's distant and responds only in monosyllables.

Once we've crossed the mixed area, we tackle the wind-sculpted snow couloir. The terrain is easier here and we can increase our pace. I drag my pole behind me and Tom grabs the end of it to follow. I am careful on the carved ice waves which occasionally form stair-like steps. I steer Tom constantly and stop him from time to time when the gap is too big.

I'm cold. Resentment overcomes me, engulfs me. What the hell am I doing in this nightmare? Why is Tom in this state? Could he not take care of himself? The situation is so unfair. Why is it always my partner who falls apart on an expedition? Why do I always have to deal with the mess? What's happened to all our rules, the ones we've always applied: self-awareness, clear-thinking, wisdom, respect for our limits and turning around at the first sign of trouble?

I sink into the abyss of the night. I turn towards Tomek. He's no longer wearing his Buff; his nose is completely white.[5] I shout: 'Tomek! Put your Buff back on over your face!'

But Tom is having difficulty breathing. He takes his Buff off once again. I stop. 'Tom, put your Buff back on – your nose is freezing.'

'Éli, I can't breathe! I'm suffocating!'

His words ricochet in my head, swirling around. Oedema? My God, maybe Tomek is suffering from the early stages of oedema? I swear into the winds; I am distraught, stunned by the rapid deterioration in his condition. Panic overwhelms me once again.

'Éli, my hands are very cold.'

I quickly get out the first aid box. I take off my gloves, take a dose of dexamethasone, a powerful corticosteroid recommended in emergencies to control cerebral oedema, and a syringe. I put my pair of mitts in my down suit to keep them warm. I try to administer the injection, but on contact with Tomek's suit, the needle breaks!

'Tom, what are you wearing under your suit?'

'My Gore-Tex – I've kept my Gore-Tex layer on.'

'Shit!'

I only have one needle in this box. It's an emergency box; the others are at Camp 4!

Then I look for the medication box and give him four 400-milligram tablets of dexamethasone, a big dose that I think appropriate to his size. I try to follow the advice my doctor gave me before leaving.

We swap gloves. Tomek is less cold. We set off again. His breathing is a bit better, but not good enough to justify the Buff. We must lose altitude as soon as possible. It's crucial.

Acute mountain sickness, pulmonary oedema – where is Tomek on this scale? I don't know exactly, but he is very ill. When the blood vessels of a vital organ, such as the lungs or the brain, swell up, the pressure increases and plasma leaks. This excessive pressure leads to coma, flooding the lungs in the event of pulmonary oedema, destroying the nervous system in a cerebral oedema. An oedema is an absolute emergency – you have to descend very rapidly in the hope that it's not already too late, because once the process has begun, the brain or the lungs are drowning. We don't have any bottled oxygen with us, which could curb the unrelenting increase in fluid and pressure in Tom's lungs.

I push and encourage him, and I fight. Flee to the bottom, run away from here. I keep talking to Tom. I don't know if he understands or if he even hears my advice. He seems lost, far off in his thoughts, far gone in his suffering. A few hours before, we were full of joy.

I control his movements and my own. My head is constantly moving back and forth, looking from below to above: in front of me —Tomek, in front of me—Tomek, in front of me—Tomek … In automatic mode once again.

My only motivation, my mantra: get back to Camp 4, then Base Camp; then get home, alive. So Tomek can return to Anna, so I can snuggle in the arms of my husband. This horizon seems so distant, and yet it's my only driving force now that everything is foundering.

I enter the descent couloir. I kick in my crampons. To guide Tomek, I again hold my pole behind me and he grabs the end. I hold my ice axe in the other hand. It's the only way to arrest a fall if Tom slips sideways. A rope would be very useful to hold him, and much more practical. But we had no reason to bring one ... barring an accident.

I realise that we are no longer following our footsteps from the ascent. We have reached the junction of the couloir and the mixed section. We continue down the steep couloir. We are moving slowly, but not too badly. I encourage Tom as much as I can. But he remains closed off, almost mute, responding only with 'yes' or 'no'.

I sink my ice axe into the hard snow. I kick in my crampons. Make a step downwards. Tom follows my pace but no longer has any axes – where have they gone?

The slope gets steeper. The reassuring white of the couloir disappears in the abyss of darkness. The bottom of the couloir is visible. The rest is difficult to discern. I set Tom down on an uncovered rock. I look for the best way through. I remember that at the bottom of the couloir there is a rocky ridge. We have to turn off before this. I set off once again, following my instinct. Ten metres lower, I spot the line of weakness. I memorise the wall and our route. I turn off my head torch and wait thirty seconds in the dark to activate my night vision. I can see the rest. It's good – the ramp will lead us back to the slope. I climb back up to Tom as quickly as possible. My legs are burning; I gasp uncontrollably. I feel like my heart will explode under the pressure I'm putting it through. I don't want to waste time; I make the most of it to warm myself up, but the pace that I'm setting is fierce.

'OK, Tom, let's go. Take my poles for ten metres. Then lean on my shoulder like at the start.'

We cross a steeper, very windswept passage, full of irregular breaks and bumps of all sizes, then the mixed zone. I have to be very careful. Sometimes I position Tomek facing the slope so that he has better support. He succeeds in downclimbing the steeper passage. I stay by his side. We move forward. We're going down. But we're still high up. I give him my hand, coordinating his movements on the next few steps. We leave this precarious zone. I dig in my axe up to the shaft. The anchor is solid. The snow accumulated here is lighter and the slope finally becomes more accommodating. We continue to traverse and descend until we reach the fixed ropes. I'm optimistic: in a few hours, we will be warm in our sleeping bags.

The freezing night wind compels me to keep active. I make big circles with my arms to warm up. What's the temperature in this wind: -50, -60° Celsius? Less? I don't know, but the wind-chill effect – the cold felt because of the freezing wind – is horrendous: never in my life have I felt such a biting cold, at the limit of my tolerance.

'Are you OK, Tom? Not too cold?'

'Yes, I'm cold!'

I rub his back energetically.

I analyse the terrain. We are high up, still too high. We have to descend as far as we can. Thanks to the very strong bond that unites us, thanks to the automated actions that we've forged as a roped team over the course of our expeditions, this descent and rescue has fallen into place naturally. Tomek is fighting. His fatigue-shattered body is degrading visibly, eaten away by the effects of the altitude and cold. His tongue freezes when he opens his mouth. When he tries to breathe, the freezing air burns his lungs and throat. I am filled with anguish. The pain that he is feeling pierces my heart. His body is nothing but suffering, and it's impossible for me to take a share of it myself to ease his struggle.

I take a deep breath and turn my gaze away from his face. Fortunately, the black night shields me from this unbearable image of Tomek. My thoughts swirl. We continue in heavy silence.

I suddenly feel very alone, lost and vulnerable.

On the slopes joining the foot of the pyramid, I shine my head torch at Tomek. His nose is completely white, eaten away by frost. Blood is flowing from his mouth. This blood terrifies me. His eyes are nothing but exhaustion, suffering, fear. I can't speak; I'm in shock. He shows me his hands, wrists curled like claws. 'Éli! I can't close them any more!' At this point, I think we both realise that his hands are lost.

At Base Camp, during our day spent waiting, Tomek had spoken to me at length about what he had experienced on Nanga in 2015, his suffering after the crevasse fall where I'd succeeded in getting him out, and his frostbitten toes. He hadn't treated them immediately, and the wounds had become infected. He had been in a lot of pain. He never wanted to relive that. 'I don't want to suffer frostbite again,' he told me. 'I need my hands for work. Otherwise I won't be able to do anything any more!'

He's so cold that he can't stop shaking. I hold him in my arms.

Tomek asks me for another tablet to keep going. At Base Camp, he had shown me a small round tablet and warned me: 'This medication, you take it when you can't go on any more.' At first I thought it was an amphetamine; but no, it's just a stimulant.

I try to reassure him. 'Tomek, we need to go down. Take my shoulder and we'll descend the fixed ropes.' I hold him because he can only brace with his arm, since his hand is unusable. This section is a traverse. To be extra safe, I clip him in with his karabiner. I secure myself too, and we arrive at the end of the fixed ropes. Tom is depleted. 'Tom, every metre travelled is a victory; the camp is getting closer. Come on, big guy!' My mind is blank. I have to concentrate on the next bit, move forward, but I can't do it. I see only Tomek's face; I can't get this horrible image out of my head. For God's sake, do something!

I realise that we're not going to reach the tent. We're at an altitude of 7,522 metres. We can descend, but not traverse and ascend towards the Diama glacier. Tom can't do it; he can't go on any longer. We are caught in the trap, this trap that had posed such a challenge for me at Base Camp and that we had discussed at such length. Deep down, I know that if we sit here, it's over: we won't be able to leave.

The blood flowing from Tomek's mouth panics me. If I can't do anything for him here, he will freeze and become a prisoner of Nanga. We have always managed on our own; we set off fully aware of the risks that we were taking in choosing alpine style, the most stripped-down type of ascent. But now, in spite of our principles, I have to do everything in my power to get him out of the clutches of Nanga. I have to send an SOS – it's my duty; this is a vital emergency for Tom. I am breaking the code, our code, but I'm afraid for him, for his life.

11.10 p.m. I send a message to my husband, and a distress call to Ludo:

> *Tomek need rescu soon frosbite and he didn't see nothing pleas manage something with ali sonner as you can. Altitude: 7,522m.*[6]

I also send a message to Anna and to Altaf, the Pakistani soldier who is at Base Camp.

Ludo answers immediately:

> *OK.*

Something changes inside me. I am no longer alone in helping Tomek. Jean-Christophe, Anna and Ludo are with me. A ray of hope in the face of Tom's traumatised appearance. I think back to discussions with Tom, Ali and Daniele on the subject of rescues in Pakistan and the altitudes reached. Reconnaissance flights above 7,000 metres on Gasherbrum I and on the Mazeno Ridge have been successful. But to land a helicopter? Carry out a rescue? With this wind and these temperatures? I talk to Tom. We are too high; we must descend. I wait for news from Ludo.

Jean-Christophe sends me a comforting message and informs me that Ludo will be the one supervising our exchanges in order to save battery on my inReach and avoid duplicating information. Ludo will be the link between Europe, Pakistan and me.

I feel less alone. I find a little energy for both of us. After the terrible image of Tom and his frostbite, I can move on to an image of hope, for a fraction of a second, a very small fraction. Release the pressure inside my head a little. We are no longer fighting completely alone on this mountain. Anna sends positive vibes to Tomek; Jean-Christophe carries me with his tender and confident words; Ludo guides and informs me.

Even if we are very alone here, in the freezing cold, in the terrifying silence of the night, I no longer feel so isolated.

New message from Ludo:

*We are organising that don't take any risks descend if necessary.*[7]

I respond immediately:

*Thanks it's shit here I'm freezing outside and I'm really scared for Tomek.*[8]

I resume the descent with Tom. The terrain is easier and, what's more, I can attach us to the fixed ropes. I hold Tom by the elbow. I don't want to hurt his frozen hands. I talk to him about the rescue that Ludo is organising. But we both know that we are still far too high to be met by a helicopter.

I can move forwards while getting Tom down and read the messages from Ludo. But I can't reply to them. Removing my gloves is impossible. My fingers freeze in five seconds.

Ludo tries to reassure me. 11.27 p.m.:

*Am on phone to Ali. He's trying to organise this. certain 100% avail tomorrow morning.*[9]

But, one minute later, a new message:

*Can you descend alone? Trying to look at other rescues besides Ali.*[10]

Fifteen minutes pass. Tom is exhausted; he needs to take a break. I sit him down on the crest of a wave of snow. He can't squat by himself any more. He holds his head against me and I shield him from the wind. I don't understand Ludo's message. Leaving Tom behind is unthinkable! I triggered a rescue for him, but it's not me who's in danger, it's him! We have to help him, to get him back down as quickly as possible. Why is Ludo talking to me about descending alone?

I write:

*I am not leaving Tom.*[11]

*alone for me that's really risky big glacier and too far tom.*[12]

I shut down the suggestion by making the argument that the glacier is impossible. Full stop. Tom is the priority.

I turn off the inReach. 'Come on, big man, here we go. We have to keep moving, or we won't be able to hold out. You have to move, Tom. Come on!' He doesn't move. 'Come on, my Tom! Come on!' I help him get back on his feet. He suffers, he moans. I pray inside. I pray that they will come to his rescue, for his suffering to be relieved. I clip Tom's karabiner to the fixed rope to connect his harness to the rope by his sling, thereby keeping him safe in case of a fall. The fixed rope is visible, resting on the snow, and is usable. Unbelievable luck in the middle of winter! We continue our descent.

The snow is once again well-sculpted and polished by the wind. My head torch reveals a wave a good metre in height. I help Tom down, but I can barely support his weight. Two steps later, we have to painfully reascend this metre. The step up is almost impossible for Tom. I cut steps with my crampons and stomp down hard on them to flatten a comfortable platform for Tom. I am facing him, bent double, and supporting him under both shoulders. I pull with all my might. In vain. He can't push on his front points with his feet.

I'll have to go about it differently. I descend. I hack steps with my ice axe. I hope that the steps are large enough to fully support him. Tom sits down while he waits. Head down, he has his arms folded against his chest and his knees are bent against his arms. 'Tom! Tommm!' His head lifts up slowly. A trickle of frozen blood hangs from his bottom lip and ends in red-tinged crystals on his beard. Time stops. One moment, an eternity. My heart is racing; it's beating so fast that I feel as though I can hear it. I squat down beside Tomek. I put my left hand on his head and slide the right under his right arm, level with his armpit. I rest his head against mine. My forehead leans on his hood. I stay silent, shocked by the atrocity of the situation. Tom murmurs between his jaws, frozen by the cold, 'Éli, I can't go on any more. I have to stop. I have to rest.'

I realise that I have to find a solution. It's not like in 2015, when

I managed to pull him out of a crevasse and get him down. Tomek is in such a state of exhaustion that he can no longer move forward. He's saying very little, he's breathing with difficulty and blood is running from his mouth on to his beard, his clothes. His feet and his hands are causing him to suffer terribly. He's exhausted.

'OK, Tom, I'm going to look for a shelter hole. We're too exposed to the wind and the cold; we have to shelter. But first, we need to get over this little wall of ice. I'll find something behind it, don't worry.' I know I'm asking a superhuman effort of him.

I struggle to stand him back up; he staggers, gives up. He seems so lost, so deep in suffering and resignation. He doesn't really react any more. I wrap my arms around him, support him and explain the process once again. 'Tom, I'll stay behind you. You have three steps to take. I'll push you from behind. Don't worry, I won't let go.' I turn him near the wall. Raise his left foot, place it on the step. 'Tom, you push on your left foot and I'll help you to stand up. One, two, three, goooo!' Tom stands up. I have just enough time to wedge his buttocks on my shoulder. 'Shift your weight forward, Tom! Shift your weight!' He rocks forward and relieves my shoulder. I can take his right foot and position it on the second step. 'Come on, push on your right foot, Tom. Push, Tom! The right.' He is leaning on the snow. Both feet anchored in the steps. 'Tom, move your weight to the right! To the right, Tom!' He doesn't manage it. 'Lift this side, Tom; lift up your leg, where you feel my hand.' The load shifts. I can grab his foot and place it on the last step. This one is more straightforward. The incline of the slope leads him to place his right knee directly on to it. I help him by pushing his back. Kneeling in the snow, he slumps down, chokes, groans. I shake frantically every which way to warm up a bit. I am so cold. My feet, trapped in the aluminium sheets which I never should have put on, are frozen!

The thirty metres below us are easier; Tomek will be able to descend alone while I go and explore the terrain. I clip him back on to the rope and explain the next part.

'Tom, I will go and look down below. You can descend, the terrain is smooth. There are no waves. The rope is tight. Hold it between your arms and follow it.' A sound leaves his mouth. Not a yes nor a no nor an OK. Just a sound.

I descend. I inspect a few crevasses, but they are unusable. I continue to downclimb and, about a hundred metres lower, I find one with an easier entrance, facing the Diamir side. I explore it and see a small cave in which we could shelter. I go back up to get Tomek. He's sitting in the snow, exhausted. Hands crossed against his chest, knees bent and head bent above his knees. He hasn't moved. I stand him up, support him. He staggers, but he's walking. Thank God!

I bring him down into the crevasse by holding on to his arms. But he's too heavy and I'm too small, not strong enough to hold him this way. He slips through my hands. I can't do anything – he's falling! Fortunately, he doesn't fall far: a metre and a half at most. A mattress of snow absorbs his landing. He finds himself flat on his back on the little terrace. He doesn't slide towards the black mouth of the crevasse. I join him and put him back on his feet. I take off my small rucksack, spread it out on the ground and we sit on it, finally sheltered from the wind. Tom lies on my bent knee. I support his back with my other straightened leg. His head is resting on my thigh.

He says nothing, shivering. I take him in my arms, talk to him, but he doesn't respond. He has closed his eyes, so I let him rest. He's exhausted. I keep him in my arms. It's around 4 a.m. and we are at an altitude of 7,282 metres. Suddenly, finally, I feel the warmth between us. I hear only Tom's jerky breathing and a breeze of air, its course blocked by the lip of the crevasse. I know that time is running out, that every minute counts. That hope for Tom can only come from heaven. He drew on his last atom of strength to descend this far, but the frostbite has cemented his face, his hands, his feet. The expression on his face is dreadful. Tom has been beyond his limit for so long. The situation weighs me down.

That night, I witnessed one of the most terrifying and moving displays of courage and tenacity that a human being can demonstrate in order to survive.

I feel suffocated in this crevasse. I have pins and needles in my legs under the pressure of Tom's upper body. I need to go out. I lie Tomek on the rucksack, reposition his hood over his head and his traumatised face, and go back up. Poised on the snowy ramp, I turn on the inReach and find a message from my husband. His words touch me deeply.

A message from Anna too, reassuring, soothing:

*Tomek will survive. Do everything you can for him but I have confidence in him, I have confidence in you, in both of you.*[13]

And again:

*It will be fine, Eli, Organizing heli, organizing help.*

*Eli, will be fine please help him! do you have medicine?*

I respond to her:

*yes we have medicine, we already use dexa and other medicin. But will be great if tomorrow he can fly. Im worri about him. Anna I'm doing my best for him, and my friend organiz rescu for him.*

Anna again:

*thx you. Me too. What can I do?*

*Tomek will be fine, don't worry. He will be ok. He will survive.*

*I trust in Tom, in you, in both of you.*

I respond:

*Thx Anna. I'll share all your positive vib for Tom.*

Some words from Ludo, too, on what has been organised:

*Helicopter Ok between 10 and 11 descend to the max. Thinking of you. Love. Drink eat move.*[14]

*We are trying ground rescue too. Embassy. Army. Heli. You're not alone. Go down.*[15]

I lie on the sloping ramp of snow, below the entrance to the crevasse, just above Tomek. The mountain is still weighed down by the burden of night. I watch the sky; my gaze shifts to the stars that inspire me. I'm cold – an arctic wind hits my face, freezes my cheeks, numbs my thoughts and my senses. I can't stand to look at Tomek's face any more: his frozen nose, the blood running from his mouth. I need to isolate myself here and think. How am I going to be able to help him? What state will he be in in a few hours? A rescue at this altitude is beyond complicated, especially when there are two of us. Alone, I will no longer be able to do anything if Tom can't put one foot in front of the other. A deep despair takes hold of me.

All night long, fraught with worry, I'm unable to sleep. Anxiety polarises and electrifies my thoughts. The icy wind cuts into me. Blades of ice whip my face; the snow creeps in everywhere.

Minutes, hours go by, indistinct. I don't know whether time is passing quickly or dragging slowly. I get angry with myself. I re-read Ludo's messages but can't work out the timeline.

> Climbers from K2 comes with 1 heli in case of. 2nd heli will
> collect you where you are. Share me position.[16]
> We try ground rescue too. Embassy. Army. Heli.[17]

I respond curtly:

> Great I am freezing am at edge of crevasse limit of frostbite will
> send you my GPS position tomorrow.[18]

It's 5.30 a.m. I turn off the inReach.

I can see the dawn looming. Nanga's shadow takes shape on Ganalo Peak. The horizon is painted with pink powder; the peaks light up one by one while the stars vanish. It's spectacular. The dawn revives my frozen, numb body. I slap my thighs and rub my muscles vigorously.

# 26 JANUARY 2018

A new day begins. I have to look after Tom while we wait to be rescued. He is cold, thirsty. I need to return to Camp 4 to recover a few things: the stove, a mat, the tent, a sleeping bag. I go back down into the crevasse; he is dozing. 'Tom, Anna is thinking of you with all her heart. She has faith in you. She sends you all her love, her warmth and comfort. You are not alone, Tom; she is with you, near you. Ludo, Anna, Jean-Christophe are working to get us out of here.' I tell him that the rescue efforts are being organised.

But in reality, the messages I've received are very vague and I have trouble understanding the arrangements. Ludo informed me at 1 a.m. that helicopters would leave at about 10 or 11 a.m. *Descend to the max*, he had added.[19] But two hours later, he told me about an additional ground rescue, while asking me to descend. Around 5 a.m., he mentioned climbers from K2 …

I repeat to Tomek: 'I'll go and look for our camp to bring back the sleeping bags, some food, the stove. The rescue is being organised. Anna loves you and is thinking about you very deeply.' He responds only with 'Yes.' I check he's not too cold. 'No.' Leaving him alone here means putting him at risk, but I need to fetch something to protect him, to help him.

I climb out of the crevasse. I navigate across the endless Bazhin Hollow, a patchwork of giant crevasses and breaks more than two kilometres in length, looking for Camp 4. When we set it up two days ago, on 24 January, we were in a blizzard and I wasn't able to spot any landmarks on the arête. Nor did we mark the placement of the tent, as we planned to retrace our ascent tracks.

A few hundred metres after leaving, I turn around suddenly. The crevasse! I haven't marked the crevasse where Tomek is sheltering with my pole to signpost the entrance! How could I be so stupid? I've been immersed in my thoughts and I broke a basic rule of thumb. I retrace my path with my eyes. I read my crampon marks in the snow and follow them back up to their origin. I see the fixed rope. It's OK: the rope is there and the crevasse is five metres below it. The unique entrance leaves no doubt. I commit the image to memory. Phew!

I continue. For more than two hours, I search, I explore each crevasse, I run all over the place. In vain. I'm at the same altitude as when we left the camp, but everything looks the same; there are hundreds of entrances like the opening of the crevasse where we bivouacked the day before. Why didn't we mark it? I need to get back to Tomek; it's been too long since I left him.

I wander on this plateau. I feel drained, devastated, shocked by what has happened since the summit. I am dumbfounded by Tomek's state; I can't get the excruciating image of his face, of his hands, out of my mind. I lose my instinct, can't concentrate any more. Usually in the mountains, my head works like a miniature GPS. Once I've passed somewhere, I know how to retrace my steps. It has never failed me before. I've never got lost, even in fog. Never. But today, I can't detach myself from my emotions in order to focus on the surroundings. My thoughts revolve around Tomek in a continuous loop.

I'm not far from our Camp 4, but I can't find it. I keep looking, alternating between contour lines, widening the circle.

10 a.m. A message from Ludo:

*Are you at the tent? Situation you tomek. Might have to descend a bit for the heli.*[20]

Desperate, angry with myself because I haven't found the camp, I try once again. I will head to the start of the ridge, where we arrived from Camp 3. This way I'll find the crevasse entrance to our tent more easily. I hover at the altitude of Camp 4, which is at 7,300 metres according to the inReach, and cross the glacier plateau for about two kilometres. I say plateau, but there's nothing flat about it. It's tilted at about thirty degrees at this altitude. Again and again, fifty metres from an entrance, I say to myself: this is it! Illusion, deception. But this time, I'm sure of it: the shape is identical, the surroundings too! In front of the entrance, the hole is blocked. It's not our crevasse! At this moment, Ludo asks me to share my GPS position for rescue. 7,386 metres. I share it.

I curse myself. It's the only camp of the whole climb that's inside a crevasse. The only one. We were able to spend a less harsh night inside, protected from the wind and cold by this natural shelter. I'm going round in circles, I'm getting angry, I'm going crazy. The effort is suffocating.

I have to return to the crevasse where I left Tomek; he's been alone for too long. On the way, I exchange several messages with Ludo and Jean-Christophe.

I'm back at the crevasse. I share my position so that Ludo has the exact location of our makeshift shelter: 7,282 metres.

I descend to find Tomek. He tells me that he's cold. He's still bleeding. His face has changed: his chapped skin is frozen deep, his eyes are glassy. He's disfigured. I see that he's missing a glove; he's put some sort of plastic around his hand, I don't understand what's happened, what he wanted to do. His hand is closed, his clenched fist so white. On the other hand, he is still wearing the mitt that I gave him. But there's blood everywhere – on his beard, on his clothes.

12.17 p.m. I send another message

*Tomek is in a terrible state, can't walk, couldn't find the tent but need evac asap.*[21]

Then another, at 12.44 p.m.:
*wind picking up and Tomek bleeding a lot from frostbite,
infection won't take long. Altitude 7,273 m.*[22]

I take my last spare pair of gloves out of my little bag. I slip the mitt over Tom's bare hand. I leave the clear plastic on. His hand is cold, hard, frozen. Fortunately, my pair is a large size and I can fit his whole hand inside. Why is he missing a glove? I don't want to tire him with my questions.

He's too cold. I have to get him back up into the sun. I'll cut a length from the fixed ropes that are hanging just above us. But with the adze of an ice axe, it's a long and difficult operation. The night we've just endured courses through my head. Reaching the summit. The endless descent in the dark and the chain of struggles. I try to address the situation like a mathematical equation:

1. I know the helis are on their way, but I don't know when they'll arrive.
2. I know we're no longer alone: Jean-Christophe, Ludo and Anna are managing things as best they can. But I don't know all the obstacles they're up against.
3. I know Ludo is managing the exchanges between the team he's assembled, and making the link between Nanga and Europe.
4. What are my options? I can descend the Kinshofer route, the normal ascent route on Nanga: it's unknown terrain, steep, but with no crevasses. It's possible as far as Camp 3. Beyond that, it's impossible and dangerous to go solo on sheer ice, without abseiling. Alternatively, I can traverse across the Diama, the new route that we established on 23 and 24 January: familiar terrain, doable alone, but with many crevasses and precarious snow bridges. It'll take longer to reach the required altitude, but this route offers me another chance to find the Camp 4 bivouac and something to protect Tomek until help arrives. Final option: I stay with Tom, protect him, keep him company …

I am so helpless. Terrified. We are paying the price for a chain of small decisions, little mistakes that led us to disaster. Can a miracle still happen? To keep going, to hope, that's life. I think of Jean-Christophe. I have to find a solution to get us out of here, Tom and me; to get away from the mountain, this place that has become hostile, severe and cold. We're both going to get out of it! We will be rescued and tomorrow this will be a bad memory. I pray that help will come as soon as possible; Tomek can't wait any longer. The weather is good, at least; helicopters can fly. What about me? What should I do? Can I leave it a few hours? Should I descend? Stay with him and wait? I can't leave him. I'm torn. My situation is not hopeless; I still don't understand why Ludo asked me to go down!

> I will only learn of the rescue organisation, the crowdfunding launched by Masha Gordon to fund it, the scale of the operation, the complexity of the negotiations, etc., long after my return.
>
> In the months that followed, I met many people who were involved, in one way or another, in the rescue organisation in France, Poland, Pakistan and Italy. Daniele Nardi, thanks to his knowledge of the mountain and his network of acquaintances in Italy and in Pakistan, played a crucial role. The rescue team was formed of more than thirty people, via a WhatsApp group, and they spent seventy-five hours non-stop behind their computers phoning, studying, deciding, organising, managing, negotiating and coaching, with Ludo coordinating all these efforts from Gap.
>
> Last February, at the ISPO show in Munich, I met an Italian who told me: 'I'm sorry, Éli, I was one of the many people who pushed and strained for you to get down and be here today. I know the consequences this had for you, but we had to save you and convince you to escape from that mountain.'

I descend into the crevasse. Tom is frozen. I rub his thighs and back gently. I'm afraid of hurting him. I tie him in with the length of rope that I finally sheared with the adze of my ice axe. I pull the rope back up and make a belay with my ice axe to try a hauling system, but the snow is too inconsistent for a solid anchor. I have to dig underneath, lie my axe flat at the bottom. Place a sling in the centre, cover it with snow and extract the sling. Here, I have a solid anchor point. I place a karabiner on the sling and pass the rope through it. I tie an Italian hitch knot and add some cord for hauling. I get Tomek tight at the end of the rope to haul him up. He can't put weight on his feet; he's sitting on his knees. Despite the weight redistribution, Tomek is still heavy. I pull with all my strength. But I can't lift him; I have to use an ascender. Suddenly, I feel the tension decrease on the strand of rope. Tom is helping me! He managed to relieve the rope by bracing his knees on the steps I had carved. After a long time – I have lost my sense of time, one hour, maybe two? – I manage to extract him from the crevasse. I lie him on his side, in the sun on the snow slope.

I do what I can to position Tomek comfortably; I raise his head so he can breathe better and hold it in my lap. His voice has changed: it's hoarse, awful, like it was in 2015, after he fell into the crevasse. As though he was from another world. He's thirsty, trying to swallow his saliva in pain. I have no water. It's been twenty-four hours since we emptied our water bottles, just below the summit. I pick up a bit of snow on the tips of my fingers and put it in his mouth. He lets it melt slowly, but the liquid runs outwards. I give him some more. Same situation. I stop. Tom is not in good shape. The glare and radiation are substantial, so I shelter his traumatised face from the sun. I am on my knees, my hand resting on his shoulder.

I talk to him. I try to reassure him and talk about something other than the rescue.

'Tomek, you reached the summit of Nanga, your life goal. You can write your book; people will help you, Anna will help you, I will help you.'

'Yes.'

We have discussed this book many times together over the last year.

We've agreed that I'll help him write the chapters about our story. We've already decided on the title: *Czapkins Life*. *Czapkins*, which means 'cap' in Polish, is Tomek's nickname. Tom always wears a cap on his head, whatever the season. *Life* is for all the lives he's already lived. As a kid in the forest with his grandmother. As an adolescent in the town, unhappy amid the concrete and tarmac. As an adult, addicted to heroin, then undergoing rehabilitation at the Monar centre in Poland. A hair's breadth from an overdose after relapsing. Another round of rehab, and he sorted himself out. He discovered the Himalaya during a trip in India, did some sailing, married Joana, had two children: Max and Tonia. He discovered rock climbing with Marek Klonowski and progressed quickly. Then, in 2008, with Marek, he spent almost forty days on the world's biggest glaciers between Yukon Territory and Alaska, and succeeded in the integral traverse of Mount Logan (5,959 metres), Canada's highest point. Then, in 2009, he climbed Khan Tengri (7,010 metres) solo in the Tian Shan massif in Kazakhstan. He went to work in Ireland, returned to Poland, met Anna. Zoïa was born. All three of them left to live in Ireland. In 2010, he discovered Nanga and her goddess, Fairy, who became the object of his spiritual quest. In December, shortly before flying to Islamabad, he told a Polish media outlet: 'This mountain will never leave me alone.' To an Italian journalist, he said that after having spent six winters in a row on Nanga, it felt a little like home there. He also spoke of the strange relationship he had established with this mountain, of his desire to complete this project, of the spiritual development which interested him more than all the records.

My helplessness infuriates me. I talk to Tom, reassure him, but I'm completely drained inside. I'm awaiting news from Ludo and the idea of descending alone doesn't sit well with me. I can't accept it. There's a very strong bond between Tomek and me; our climbing partnership is fused. Ever since our first meeting on Nanga, we've had a chemistry that I can't explain. The attraction of opposites, perhaps? We have neither the same physical constitution nor the same philosophy. Like him, I enjoy spending time at altitude, I like to soak up places; but I don't experience the affinity that Tom feels with this mountain and with Fairy, its goddess. Tom is an outsider, a great admirer of the Polish Himalayan mountaineer Jerzy Kukuczka. He sets off for the mountains with a bag of dreams rather than a rucksack of kit, with a mind of steel rather than the intensive physical preparation and constraints of an athlete. He's a free spirit; his spiritual quest on Nanga fascinates me. I do not always understand how he works: he alternates between phases of motivation and troughs of depression; he abandons a summit bid and then, almost as abruptly, plunges back into it. It's like an addiction. As though Nanga was simultaneously his outlet, his freedom, but also his prison!

Physically, we are opposites. He is heavier, more robust – eighty to eighty-five kilos, 1.70 metres – exceptionally hardy and robust with more in reserve. I'm small in size: 1.56 metres, forty-eight kilos at the start of the expedition, often forty on my return, with a metabolism that quickly consumes the little extra weight I try to build up before departure.

At altitude, he eats little, and can meditate and fast for a week; whereas I always need to eat. I devour portions of food for two! I eat more and more during the ascent. It reassures me; it's an indicator that I monitor. If I'm less hungry, it could mean that my acclimatisation isn't optimal.

He never seems to be cold, and often doesn't wear a hat or gloves. I need to stack layers; I'm more sensitive to the cold, more demanding in terms of comfort.

Tomek likes to walk slowly, in fits and starts. I like speed; I have a spritely and non-stop rhythm. Before setting off on an expedition, Tomek trains very little. 'Why would I tire myself by running?' he would often say, laughing. He likes to smoke, too. This year, for the first time, he listened to me: at home in Ireland, in the evenings after work, he trained; and above all, he quit smoking.

Me, on the other hand, I leave little to no room for chance: I prepare everything, calculate, train like an elite athlete, draw up safety protocols.

We also differ a lot in our approach to safety on expedition. He counts on Fairy to guide us. I need to calculate everything, to study the route, visualise, even if I rely a lot on my intuition on the mountain. I can feel where the crux of the route is, how to advance in the fog, in a labyrinth of ice. I memorise the details of the relief, the contours, and I am able to retrace my steps, even when it's dark or foggy. In our team, I'm the one who's most often at the front. I like looking for the way ahead, or anticipating it. I never feel lost; I am rarely scared. I study all possibilities of 'escape' in advance – analysing the descent route before reaching the summit – and set myself a maximum number of days up there, so I always calculate the time required to reach the summit and back and the time spent exposed while traversing, depending on the winds.

Tom doesn't care about the weather forecast; he doesn't want to stress about that, being convinced that Fairy is watching over him. He climbs to the rhythm of the mountain, he has said in the past. I need to know the weather forecast in advance in order to anticipate the next part. He knows he is able to spend several days at altitude waiting for the weather to calm before setting off again, to meditate, to draw on unknown resources deep within him; he feels capable of facing a storm, of retreating into an ice cave while waiting for the good weather to return – indeed, he's done it all before. Me, on the other hand, I absolutely need the weather bulletin that Jean-Christophe or Ludo send me each day, otherwise I don't feel calm. The idea of being trapped by bad weather beyond the sérac at an altitude of more than 6,000 metres in hellish winds terrifies me. Remaining stationary at altitude also means taking risks unnecessarily, losing strength and energy. I always try to preserve my energy and speed for as long as possible on the mountain in order to make another attempt if the weather thwarts us on the first push.

We differ still more in our ways of relating to our loved ones while on expedition. Every day, I keep my husband Jean-Christophe informed: it's a system we decided on together, before I left. And I dutifully respect this commitment for both our sakes. To communicate, I've carried a satellite phone, a Thuraya, which I had to leave at Base Camp, and a GPS tracker, an inReach. Inexpensive equipment. On the other hand, I have no internet connection on expedition: it's my choice to cut myself off from everything. Today's world is ultra-connected, and I feel saturated with information against my will. I like to disconnect from the news, from the pace of the world, and plug into the mountain.

Tom didn't bring any means of communication. The Thuraya that he had during the 2016 expedition has been broken since his return and he didn't get it fixed. He won't send news to his wife, Anna; he says it's not a problem. I have already discussed this with him several times. Why leave Anna in this state of uncertainty? He says it's a way of protecting her, to prove his love to her, rather than entangling her in the daily routine of his thoughts up there. I don't see it that way. If I didn't keep my husband updated, I would subject him to the anguish of being the one who waits knowing nothing, while being able to imagine everything. Fortunately, Anna is in regular contact with Jean-Christophe and as soon as I send news, he forwards it to her!

Tomek is also completely obsessed with the myth or legend of Fairy. Over the course of his expeditions on this mountain, he seems to have connected with the goddess of the mountain. When in doubt, he says, 'I'm going to talk to Fairy', before going off alone. Then he comes back and says: 'We're going to do that; we'll go through there.'

'She's a goddess who either welcomes or rejects you. You must not see her face in a dream, otherwise you will die on the mountain!' That's what the people living in the valleys around Nanga Parbat say. When Tom told me this story, I immediately thought, 'OK, this is just a medieval legend.' But he believes it; he assures me that Fairy speaks to him in his dreams, guides him.

In 2015, he was alone on Nanga, on the Rupal Face. While sitting behind a rock, he heard a voice: 'I want you, I want you!' Then an entire section of the mountain detached around him in a slab avalanche. In 2015, while falling into a crevasse: 'But what are you doing?' 'Don't worry, if he's strong he'll survive!' And Tomek survived this fall of forty, fifty metres. In 2016, we were together and struggling on a nasty overhanging sérac. I was exhausted, hacking my axes into a complicated section of ice, trying to forge a way through in a suffocating battle. I was within an inch of making it, but the ice was too delicate in the last few metres, dashing my only hope. Behind, a blade of ice stood out. We had to go and look. Tom said to me: 'Give me two minutes. I'll think about it.' In my head, I said to myself: 'OK, this is the Fairy call!' He came back: 'Éli, the way through is in the crevasse.' I agreed: 'OK, we'll try; we don't have much choice any more anyway.' The key to the section really was inside the crevasse! Tom credited this victory to Fairy. I remained doubtful.

Through his appreciation of Hindu culture, which he discovered during a long stay in a leper colony in India, Tomek is inspired by Fairy. His attempts to reach the summit of Nanga are as close to a mystical, existential quest as they are to a sporting achievement. For him, to go on the conquest of a summit is to go and conquer himself: through non-attachment, the shedding of all comfort, towards a more intense present moment, separated from the useless past, not considering the future beyond the next step … The freedom of one who has nothing. He questions modern Himalayan mountaineering and its excesses.

The things I've learnt up there with him intrigue me deeply. One day at Base Camp, Tom told me: 'When you drink a glass of water, remember that the molecules have flowed a billion times in streams and rivers, have reached oceans a thousand times, have evaporated a thousand times, have formed rain and snow. These molecules have been breathed a million times; have been sweated, spat or pissed; have constituted plant and animal organisms. These molecules have always existed, and always will exist, in one form or another, before returning to their source; and they are now in your glass so you can live. If you see this, if you act consciously while eating or drinking, you escape materiality.'

For me, meditation took the place of this inspiring poetry. But maybe I'm wrong, maybe I was wrong. Tom was walking and climbing towards Fairy, getting closer to this mystery, if not through conscious perception then by keen intuition.

Tom's first words about Fairy made me smile inside. I also believe, but in God. Fairy seems to me a far-fetched idea, but listening to his stories amuses me and opens my imagination to other horizons. Fairy underpins our conversations at Base Camp with our friends, and I am convinced that this legend was born from the fear of men, like the Loch Ness monster or the Yeti. Tomek is just a hunter of enigmas!

Curiously, despite all our differences, despite our contrasting approaches and methods, Tom is the ideal climbing companion for me. I hardly ever argue with him, but enjoy chatting, singing and dreaming ... He's also the strongest partner for Nanga. His serenity and strength reassure me, soothe me. I trust him and maybe even, sometimes, his good Fairy! I love his clown face and his expressions. With me, Tom is gentle, affable, cheerful, extremely sensitive. Life down below gives him airsickness and, like him, I find that life at altitude has a way of stopping time, pulling us out of it, bringing us back to the essential, to simplicity; and even stilling the hand of our internal clock, clearing the mind. Just like me, he is inspired by the mountains.

Together, we can talk continuously without ever being bored. Tom has said to me several times: 'With you, I could talk for hours and hours; but often, with others, I have nothing to say!' In the mountains, we steer a course between silence and an excess of words; we don't need to communicate when we walk, as though our thoughts were in harmony. But at Base Camp or in the tent, we ramble on for hours. He has a radiant generosity and wins the hearts of adults and children in the Diamir Valley. He donates equipment, clothes, shoes, even if it means stripping himself of them, as in 2015 when he gave his shoes to Altaf, a policeman who was on rotation and going up to Base Camp. Tom limped down to him, after his crevasse fall. But it had snowed in the night. The next day, his already suffering feet were refreezing.

Our complicity is rare and precious in this hostile environment. Climbing Nanga Parbat in winter with Tomek means surpassing our limits but respecting the other partner, leaving them free to live out what they're looking for.

After three expeditions together here, we are still motivated, happy. We very rarely disagree. Except when we mention the 2016 expedition to Nanga Parbat. Tomek had a lively dispute at Base Camp that winter with the Italian Himalayan climber Simone Moro. And he never recovered from the hurtful remarks made by Simone, who publicly reopened old wounds from Tomek's life. Tom keeps coming back to this story. I am sure, having experienced it myself, that suffering warps our judgement and locks us in a bitter spiral that steers us away from our personality. This year, Tomek seems changed, embittered, depressed, obsessive. Whereas, from my perspective, the trio of Txikon, Sadpara and Moro accomplishing the first winter ascent freed me, definitively quashing the tension and rivalry that I felt so keenly at Base Camp in 2016. [23]

So how could I give it up, leave Tom here for a few hours and descend far away from him, as the rescue team are asking me to do? My throat is tight. I turn my head. I don't want him to see my struggle. I grasp a piece of ice tightly to tense my body before the emotion overcomes me.

I talk to him about the rescue efforts. I tell him that I didn't find Camp 4, but explain the solution pointed out by Ludo: the helicopter can't recover two people at the altitude we are at, so I must descend as far as I can alone, so he can be rescued as quickly as possible.

'Yes, Éli, that's the solution,' Tomek answers. Then he adds: 'I'm cold. I want to rest.'

These are the last words that he uttered.

The minutes pass in a stony, haunting silence. I watch Tomek and keep thinking that I need to find Camp 4 to make his waiting conditions a little more bearable. My conscience tells me that I have to stay with him to help him, keep him company, warm him up, take care of him. My sense of reason retorts with the fact that if he still has a chance of survival and I don't go down, I'm condemning him to death.

Ludo's messages follow one after the other. 1 p.m.:

*Heli slow to arrange. We're doing everything but descend as far as poss. hold on.*[24]

*Can you descend alone as far as possible?*[25]

*If 7,200 ground team. If below heli.*[26]

*we've released 15,000 euros personally for the heli but not left yet.*[27]

The option envisaged by the Pakistani rescue team and by Ali, our agent, requires that I descend: the helicopter can only carry two people, I've been told; it will go up to rescue Tomek. As for me, I have to go down alone. But I've tossed this option back and forth in my head since this morning. I can't leave. First of all because I can't bear to leave Tomek alone for too long, and then because I can't go down the Diamir glacier alone – there are too many crevasses. I will only consider it as a last resort.

The wind picks up, Tomek is cold.

New messages from Ludo:

*Can you go via the Heisendle-Messner and descend? You have to climb back up to the col for that.*[28]

*If yes leave now.*[29]

*You must descend to 6,000. Problem with heli.*[30]

So Ludo recommends the Eisendle–Messner route, one that I know and which is less technical on the descent. I think about it. The route is very crevasse-ridden, especially for a solo descent without a rope. I'm still traumatised by Tom's fall on this part of the glacier during our descent, in 2015, fittingly without a rope. We'd said never again! And if it's necessary to go back up with the ground team, if the heli can't make it to the crevasse? It will take too long. I reply to Ludo:

> *no it's the rotten part of the glacier, sérac and big crevasse and too far Tom.*[31]

New message from Ludo:

> *where do you want to go down? We need to know to organise accordingly!*[32]

I know that the wisest and fastest option is to descend by the Kinshofer, a direct route which also has the advantage of not taking me too far away from Tomek. This is the way I have to go if Ludo gives me the green light. I write back:

> *yes I can descend the Kinshofer route; probably 6,800.*
> *Just tell me when?*[33]

Then a quarter of an hour later, a new message from Ludo:

> *Ok Kinshofer then? You need to get to 6,000 … maybe 6,500 for the heli.*[34]
> *6,800 possible with winching, keep harness on.*[35]

I'm now being told to reach an altitude of 6,700 or 6,800 metres. For the first time, I start to consider this option and tell myself: 'OK, so if I want to rescue him, I have to go down.' But if I descend, it'll be by the Kinshofer route, because there are no crevasses between Camp 3 and Camp 4 on this route, meaning that I can lose altitude quickly while not moving too far from Tomek. Beyond Camp 3, however, I won't be able to continue: the great wall of sheer ice over 500 metres high, sometimes inclined at forty-five degrees, with some even steeper sections, is impassable with the equipment I have on me. And there's also the Kinshofer wall, a 100-metre-high rock face.

Even if, by extraordinary luck, there were still any fixed ropes, they would have been ensnared by the ice. Tomek had told me that he had found fixed ropes there in winter 2012, but they were unusable because they were trapped in the ice.

Tomek no longer has ice axes; he had to drop his pair on the descent. With mine, I belay and lower him back down into the crevasse. I help him to lie down in the cave once again. I tie him off with my axes and the piece of fixed rope. I'm so scared that he will slide down into the terrifying black mouth of the crevasse! I rub him up and down again.

Ludo's messages spin round and round in my head. I try to take stock, to see clearly. He told me that the helicopters can go up and meet Tomek at around 10 or 11 a.m. Ludo also said that a ground rescue was getting underway. But who is he talking about? Some climbers from K2? Ludo doesn't want me to take risks and has repeatedly asked me to go down. I can't, and in my head, I respond to him: don't worry, Ludo, I'm not taking risks just now. I have to help Tom, full stop. Let's not talk about me but about him right now!

In another message, Ludo mentioned a second helicopter, on its way to pick us up at the altitude we're at, and asked me to share my location. Then I was told that I had to go down, that the heli organisation was dragging on but they were putting the pressure on. Then Ludo asked me if I was still in the same place, if I could go down alone – and how far – to join the ground rescue team. Later, he confirmed to me that the required funds had been released, but that the helicopter had not yet left.

Tom is plunging into torpor! I have to react, move, decide. But how can I leave him?

Today, I feel responsible for not having recognised and understood the condition Tom was in when I left him, for hiding the reality from myself.

1.54 p.m. Ludo:

> *OK descend where you feel comfortable, as low as possible. But tell us for heli.*[36]

2.02 p.m. Anna:

> *Kocham ci najdrozszy dacie rade Eli dacie rade. Pomoc nadchodzi.*[37] *Eli help is coming. You will be ok*
> *Eli are you going down?*
> *will be fine Eli*

2.07 p.m. New message:

> *rescue team say: descend to 6,000m, we pick up Tomek at 7,200m and pick you up after.*[38]

So I have to go down, I have to leave Tomek? But maybe I can go and recover some equipment beforehand, while they're finalising the detailed instructions for me. I'm obsessed with our Camp 4, where our medicines, the stove and the sleeping bags remain, the things which could relieve Tomek.

I speak to Tomek: I explain to him that I'm leaving … to look for Camp 4. 'Don't worry, Tomek; the helicopter rescue is coming in a few hours.'

Now I have to live with this last image of him, his hoarse voice and the parting hope that I gave him.

# 26 JANUARY 2018
## CONTINUED

———————

I plant one of my poles to mark the location of the crevasse where Tomek is. The rescuers also have the GPS coordinates. The first steps are a nightmare. My feet weigh a tonne. I'm afraid to move away, to leave Tom. How I wish that things had turned out differently; the situation is too complicated. Only the hope of the rescue helicopters gives me the energy to move, to fight for Tomek, for us. Rescue should arrive in two or three hours, and then I'll be picked up later, lower down.

This time round, I'm trying to explore the Bazhin Hollow in a different way. I had time to think about it while I was helping Tomek. First I reach the ridge. I remember a more prominent rock that we passed on our arrival here on 24 January. I should be able to find it. The camp is almost level, a hundred metres from this point.

But everything looks the same; I can't spot it. When we passed the ridge previously, there was too much fog; it was impossible to find real landmarks. I look, I search desperately. I swear into the wind, I get angry. I wander once again on this plateau, as though in the middle of an ocean, drowning in its infinite, unfathomable immensity. The wind has carved snow waves in the middle of the crevasses, and I don't want to sink into them. The sun floods the plateau with light. The first touch of warmth, of life, since yesterday's nightmare. But, in a few hours, the trap will close on us. My head remains torn by this dilemma: wait here with Tom or leave? What should I do?

2.30 p.m. A message from Jean-Christophe. My husband's words overwhelm me, bring me back to myself. I cry.

I read his concern, but also his love, his trust – exactly what I really need to hear from him! I dream of calling him, but it's impossible. His message acts like an electric shock; he reconnects me to reality and to my emotion. Jean-Christophe gives me the strength to descend, to leave the plateau; he reiterates Ludo's words, reassures me about the organisation of the rescue. Everyone is in agreement; I'm confident.

> Descending via the Kinshofer route is the most risky decision that I've ever taken. I knew that after Camp 3 I would be stuck in a dead end, condemned. In winter, temperatures are too low and prevent snow from sticking to the wall. The violent winds sweep and polish the rock, leaving only hard, compact ice that is difficult to penetrate with crampons and ice axe. A varnished wall. But I'd left all the appropriate equipment (abseil rope, ice screws, etc.) on the Diama glacier, after the sérac passage. I only chose this route with Tom in mind, to leave a chance for both helicopter and ground rescue.

I leave alone to tackle the Kinshofer route. This time, I'm really leaving Tomek. I'm not reassured, but I move nonetheless, attempting this one last thing in my power so we have a chance to recover and save him.

It must be 3 p.m. Although my legs and my body are taking the route down, my head and my heart remain torn between the need to descend to make rescue possible and the feeling that I'm abandoning Tomek, the pain of leaving him. I tell myself that it's only for a few hours. I already abandoned him this morning when I went to look for Camp 4. I'm leaving him alone for just a few hours, before help arrives. I insulated him well; he can fight, my Tom.

At this point, I firmly believe that the helicopters will arrive and pick us up – first Tomek, then me. I apply myself to this unfamiliar descent route and, thinking of the prospect of saving Tomek, overcome my anxiety. But not my guilt about leaving him alone.

In my head, I keep going over everything that has happened since yesterday: the fatal chain of events that led us to disaster, the entire combination of circumstances still incomprehensible. Why didn't we descend when we were ninety metres below the summit? Why did we continue despite the late hour and the onset of darkness? Why didn't we turn around when we reached the summit ridge? And why didn't I 'force' Tomek to put on his goggles? Why didn't we mark the location of the Camp 4 crevasse in order to return more easily? Why didn't I manage to find the bivouac which would have enabled me to protect Tomek and keep him warm? And why did we return to Nanga once more?

Guilt overwhelms me, drowns me.

But I have to swallow these destructive thoughts, suppress my questions, my uncertainties. The only solution for Tomek will come from the air. There's no other way. I have to listen to Ludo's instructions, and those of the rescuers. Deep down, I know I have to get to the requested altitude as quickly as possible, in the hope of saving Tom. And myself? Part of me is doubtful, another reassuring. I just know that if I stayed here, I would be with Tom – I could protect him, help him, warm him up, keep him company, be there for him. But I couldn't save him or move him or bring him back down. I still have a choice: go back up, stay with him and support him; or listen carefully to Jean-Christophe and Ludo, go down and keep the options open for ground rescue or helicopter rescue for Tomek. If I stay here, I condemn him, and perhaps condemn us. If I go down, I condemn myself to a future – or contingent future – that already scares me. I feel as though I'm in an unnavigable counter-current in the middle of a storm of questions, on the brink of shipwreck, being carried along for many hours, not knowing where to find calmer shores so that I don't fail, drown and sink the boat! I wish I didn't have to decide, to descend, to leave Tom, to think any more, to distance myself from him; but this option does not exist. A rescue at 7,280 metres? Impossible for two people.

I have to help Tom, not deprive him of his only chance. I mustn't torment myself with worry. But deep down, I don't want to leave him alone. My sense of reason takes over, tries to chart the most intelligent course to weather the storm. Don't sink, navigate around difficulties, reinforce the ship. Don't give up, persevere, believe and keep my impatience in check. I decide. I will take Ludo's advice: follow the Kinshofer route until Camp 3, endeavour to get to an altitude of 6,800, 6,700 or 6,600 metres. Save Tom and banish my demons. It's not straightforward, nor is it over yet.

In my head is a litany, a mantra: 'Descend—rescue Tom—life … descend—rescue Tom—life … descend—rescue Tom—life … '

I have to descend to the requested altitude as quickly as possible so as not to delay the rescue operation for Tomek. He can no longer move. I can't carry him on my back. I can't drag him either. I feel up to facing the unknown of the descent. It's the right choice. A difficult choice that I never would have made without this hope of help, without the reassuring words of Anna, Jean-Christophe and Ludo, who sent me at least ten messages to convince me to go down. I turn off the inReach. I need to conserve battery. I have to go down the crevassed glacier until I get to a flat part. I follow the rocks as much as possible to avoid the holes. The slope then becomes less steep and the crevasses less numerous. I move away from the shoulder and deviate to the right. My focus is a red tent abandoned by a climbing team. I spotted it on the evening of the 24th, and today it has caught my eye several times. This is the classic placement for Camp 4 on the normal route. After that? I've no idea of the route I'll be able to take. The slope plunges towards the Diama. I've observed it many times from Base Camp: the route winds its way from left to right in the upper part before linking two or three mixed sections between the slopes. These passages should be downclimbable. According to climbers, the rest is a gentle slope where snow accumulates during heavy snowfall. Sometimes you have to swim through waist-deep snow. But this winter, there has been little

At the start of the Mummery Spur, 5,600 metres.

On the Mummery Spur, ascending towards 6,000 metres in windy conditions, but sheltered from any real dangers.

Daniele Nardi on the Mummery Spur, at 6,300 metres heading towards the Bazhin Hollow.

## JANUARY 2015

At 6,500 metres on the Diama glacier. Tomek is carrying a heavy load during our eight-day self-supported trek. He is a force of nature.

## JANUARY 2016

On the Diama glacier at an altitude of around 6,200 metres where I shared a sunset with Tomek that I'll remember for the rest of my life.

In Chilas during my strolls to the Indus while waiting for the paperwork to go through.

## JANUARY 2018

Sunset on Nanga, just before the long three-week jet stream period.

Nanga from our Base Camp at Kutgali.

Tom at the col linking the Diamir Valley to the Diama glacier. After this point, we no longer had visual contact with Base Camp. The route is committing and far away from everything.

**Above:** Tomek on the sérac passage at 6,200 metres. View of Ganalo Peak.

**Left:** Sérac passage at 6,200 metres which gives access to the slopes and upper Diama glacier.

**Below:** Bivouac at 6,600 metres on the Diama glacier. View of the Hindu Kush and Afghanistan.

**Top:** 24 January 2018. Sunrise at 7,300 metres. But we're not leaving straight away: Tomek's feet are too cold to continue. We return to the tent to light the stove and heat up Tomek's boots, insoles and feet before leaving for the summit.

**Above:** At 6,900 metres on 23 January 2018. Happy to have been able to advance this afternoon, after the period of violent winds in January and more than forty hours spent in the tent at 6,600 metres being tormented by savage gusts.

**Left:** Me on the traverse between the Diama glacier and the glacier between Camp 3 and Camp 4 on 24 January 2018 at 7,200 metres.

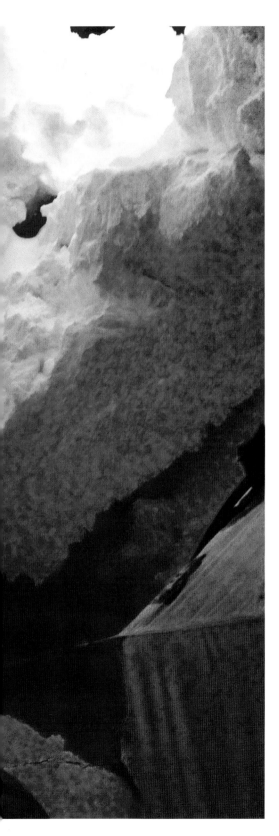

**Left:** Bivouac in the crevasse on the night of 24–25 January 2018 at 7,350 metres.

**Top:** 25 January 2018, 5.15 p.m. Final image before the summit climb. We are at 8,036 metres.

**Middle:** The real start from our bivouac in one of the crevasses on the hollow at 7,350 metres on 25 January 2018. Me in selfie and Tom behind setting off slowly in the morning.

**Bottom:** Makeshift bivouac at 6,800 metres on the morning of 27 January. Waiting on a rescue for Tomek.

28 January 2018. With Adam on the Kinshofer wall (photo taken by Denis). A happy mess of nylon on a normal route, yet one which has rarely been equipped since 2013. These infamous ropes …

Thanks, Tomek,
for being what you were.

precipitation and a strong three-week jet stream has swept everything away.

I'm moving fast. I even catch myself running in these easy descending sections. I hurry to reach the necessary altitude. I want to reach it without delay to get Tom out of this hell. It's the only thought that occupies my mind. I reach the tent. Next objective: the shoulder to my extreme right. I up my pace once again, but I'm no longer running. A flat traversing ramp reminds me that I am still in the high mountains. I'm short of breath. Old footprints mark the way. How are they still visible; how have they been able to resist the passage of wind, sun and snow? The weather has been clement this year, with little snowfall during autumn and early winter. Maybe that's why the ropes aren't trapped in the ice up there. I make ephemeral tracks which will disappear, my connecting thread in this unknown terrain. A real godsend in this vast landscape.

It's a new stage for me. I have to remember each detail of the descent in case I need to climb back up. I don't know what will follow or how life will continue in a few hours. Descending alone, walking without Tomek, feels beyond strange. Disconcerting. I turn around regularly to retrace my steps, noting significant features: this big boulder to the left, that slope to the right.

3.57 p.m. I turn on the inReach. Message from Ludo:

*send me your position and which route you choose to descend.*
*Ideally 6,700 for heli.*[39]

I send my altitude – 6,981 metres – and the GPS coordinates. And I turn off the inReach.

The traces of life are still showing me the path to follow, the right direction. I only have one pole to descend with. I hold it with both hands, push down on it and always plant it upslope as a safety measure. I should have made Tom's belay with just one point of protection and kept one of my axes! If I slip, I'm not sure that this solitary pole will be able to arrest my fall. But I was so scared that Tom would topple over into the pit of the crevasse. Nonetheless, I'm furious about my choice. I berate myself: 'Watch out! Slow down! Concentrate!' I curse myself.

4.12 p.m.:

*The helis are getting ready. Either for today or for tomorrow.*[40]
*You're doing great. Stay positive. We'll try to send one this evening with tent etc. If not tomorrow 100%.*[41]

I've just switched on the inReach again and discovered this message from Ludo which frightens me: why is he talking about tomorrow? I don't understand what's holding them up. The weather is fine here. The wind has calmed. A heli can fly well in these conditions! And that's what I've been told for hours. What's going on? It's the first time Ludo has mentioned a take-off tomorrow. Why now? Why didn't he tell me anything about this on the plateau before I changed course to descend?

I reply:

*I am without tent 3nights no sleep 24h no food, no drink, Tom worse danger.*[42]

My head hammered by questions, but still full of hope, I continue my descent to Camp 3. I trust Ludo, I know he's managing it as best he can.

4.17 p.m. Ludo:

*Doing everything we can. Hold on a bit longer. will keep you posted as soon as they decide.*[43]

4.30 p.m.:

*Position 6,671m.*

I've reached the altitude they asked for, and it's still daylight. I'm sitting on a rock waiting for the heli.

The light is fading. The sky turns orange above the mountains of Afghanistan; the sun shines on the slopes below. I have no more news. I feel fragile, like an alien on the mountain, in the world. Waiting. I struggle to control my thoughts. I'm clinging on to Tomek, sending him all my energy and my hope, I stifle my doubts deep down inside. Yesterday, the mountain was still warm and human, radiating beauty and warmth; now Nanga has become cold and hostile. I pray that time will stretch tonight and the sun won't set.

5.48 p.m. Ludo again:

*2 heli with team, arrival scheduled tomorrow at 12.30 p.m. 1.15 p.m.*[44]

*Monêtier when you get back. We love you.*[45]

Le Monêtier-les-Bains, near Briançon, is where Ludo and I like to go and recharge after an exhausting climb in the High Alps: he's trying to lift my spirits.

*you must stay at C3, there is DZ.*[46]

DZ for *drop zone*: it is in fact one of the rare places on the Kinshofer route where a flat, terraced area can be found, enabling a helicopter to land without winching.

*If you decide otherwise tell us. Good luck.*[47]

The helis won't arrive until tomorrow? Everything collapses once again inside me; it's an additional, terrible shock. I'm going to have to spend another night outside, on this mountain? But it will be excruciating, extreme! Here, alone, without equipment? Or even with Tomek in the crevasse if I manage to get back up? Two equally preposterous options, each one as perilous as the other! I feel lost, abandoned, dazed ...

I run out of patience; I explode with incomprehension. I vent my anger now. I let it all out. And curse myself a few minutes later: 'You are so useless! Why did you descend? Why did you trust the others? Shit!' My brain boils, heats up. The situation is dramatic. I'm caught in the trap that I wanted to avoid; I rushed into this!

The cold is polar, the wind bitterly cold. I don't know what to think any more. I scream my distress into the wind. I pray that my voice will reach Tom, that this sound will follow the cloudy swirls and intertwined lines which separate me from him. That the echo will slip into folds of air, sail between the layers of ice. I want Tomek to hear and respond to me so much! But the sound escapes and trails off in the wind. The storm picks up and swirls around my perch. I'm besieged from right to left, from top to bottom. I'm lost, washed up in an ice desert, deluged by forty-eight hours of pure madness.

How could this all have happened? A minor detail turned everything upside down. Was it the schedule? The decision we made at 5 p.m., at 8,035 metres, to continue towards the summit, which prompted Tomek's vision problem, the altitude that caused an oedema, the exposure to too much cold? I don't know, but I regret this decision.

I am caught between reason – along with Ludo telling me to stay here – and the desire to climb back up to Tomek. I reread the message. The helicopters will arrive tomorrow around noon. If I go back to Tomek, will I have time to come back down by midday tomorrow? But it's late. My head torch has run out of battery. I risk getting lost. I want to join Tom, but my conscience pins me down here. Ludo implores me not to go back up. In the end, I dissuade myself from doing it. But a terrible feeling of guilt overwhelms me again …

I am lost, bitter, disillusioned and above all alone, far away from Tomek. The cold numbs my feelings, which are already distorted by fatigue. I have to protect myself, concentrate, manage on my own. I don't know how I'm going to be able to get through the night. I know that it will be terrible and I pray that time might be cut short and the sun might rise quickly. That the torments of the night might be as brief as possible. It's another great irony that what I seek and appreciate on an expedition is precisely this: taking the time to live fully, with my heart and soul! This time which, down below, slips through my fingers relentlessly. I come here to take stock of my life, to evaluate distance and space with my steps, to feel with my own resources, my energy.

But this evening, time scares me, worries me. I know it will work against me. I would like to run away, but you can't escape time. When you're afflicted by the cold, dreading the depths of negative temperatures, time no longer moves forward. It slowly breaks down and plunges me into hell. I can't control the despair that overwhelms me. I can't calm myself down. I feel abandoned, betrayed, worn out. How is Tomek faring in these atrocious, freezing temperatures that have been gradually paralysing him, irreparably, for many hours now?

I have to focus my thoughts on the coming night: how to survive, how to protect myself from the wind. On these rocks, I'm just going to die. I don't have a shovel, so I can't dig a hole to shelter in. I need to find shelter. I wander through the rocks, exploring the area, but there is nothing. Nothing to keep me from the wind and the night. The sheer ice under my feet forces me to refocus on action. What if I were to cut off one of the bits of rope I've followed until now? Could I make a coil to lie on and insulate myself from the snow? Without an ice axe, this would be almost impossible. And my knife is at Camp 4! I continue. I glimpse a piece of plastic. It must be a leftover tent. It's tiny, but if I find a bigger one, I could insulate myself from the ice. I arrive at the end of the fixed rope. A small coil of rope is attached to it. I try to pull it off. In vain. I take a protruding rock to shear the rope. I hold the strand against the wall. The wind freezes my fingers immediately; I curse! These ropes can break like glass: in 2016, on Nanga's Kinshofer couloir, Adam Bielecki arrived at a belay, pulled on a fixed rope, hung on it, and the rope broke. He fell sixty metres. Today, this rope is resisting my efforts!

This bit of tent and these ropes are signs of life around here. I'm just arriving at the location of Camp 3, in fact. Under the rocky tower, I see a flat area: it's a shovelled-out terrace for a tent, a bivouac area for mountaineers. But I only see one. Maybe I'm not at the true Camp 3, but a bit above it? Sometimes, in the Himalaya, the camps teem with people during the season. So some mountaineers isolate themselves a bit higher to get some peace or even just some space. I continue my descent. I need to go and see if there's another tent or a bit of some-thing to keep myself warm tonight. A hundred metres below, several terraces confirm my suspicions. I look for a piece of fabric, a peg, a pole, the slightest 'tool' to insulate myself from the icy ground, which will be my worst enemy. Nothing. The mountain is exceptionally clean here. I stop above a terrace and notice that there are crevasses below. I need to explore – there's sure to be a crevasse that can accommodate me tonight. I could wall myself inside it. Further to the left, the slope steepens, which means more breaks, so greater chances of finding a shelter.

I follow a terrace giving access to the 'welcoming' mouth of a crevasse a few metres below, at an altitude of around 6,770 metres. The terrain is steep and the ice slippery. I downclimb the passage facing the wall and teeter along a narrow and delicate three-metre traverse. It looks thin underneath. A bridge? I approach, look, test. It's good. A little wall of ice fifty centimetres high conceals, to the right of the gaping hole, a long and narrow shelf, sixty or seventy centimetres by a metre and a half. But I don't like what I see to the left of the wall: a precarious stack of half-collapsed snow/ice which with my weight alone would disappear into the abyss. Between layers of carved concretions, a black background opens on to infinity. I place both hands on the little wall of blue-tinged ice and put my head into the lion's mouth.

After an acrobatic step, I find myself inside, finally isolated from the wind. I'm shaking like a leaf. Kneeling down, I stick my hands under my armpits to get my circulation back. I contract my back and abs to wake them up. My shoulders are tense. I rub my hands up and down my sides aggressively. And I rock my body back and forth. I stay in this position for a good while before the tremors deign to let me breathe properly. I raise my head and hit the 'ceiling', which causes snow to fall on top of my down suit; flakes end up on my neck. I curse. The freezing snow seeps into my skin. I look around. I will be able to shelter in this cramped space, sit down and eventually lie down. In this moment, I feel as though I'm between two worlds: one icy and open on the glacier and the Mazeno Ridge; the other petrifying, rising from the unfathomable depths of the abyss; both ready to snatch me in my sleep. I should stay awake all night, but I won't manage that! This crevasse is a sieve.

11.06 p.m. Ludo:

*Keep holding on the night is long but ultimately very short compared to the life that awaits you.*[48]

I read this message then turn off my inReach. Ludo's words don't calm me down.

My thoughts keep coming back to Tomek; I can't detach myself for more than fifteen minutes. Only the moments when I have to concentrate on an action allow me to escape, to stop seeing his bloody face. I am terrified by what he is living through, by our situation. Yesterday, I thought I had spent the most terrible night. Tonight I have to – *we* have to – start all over again. How did I get to this point? Why did Ludo ask me to descend if he wasn't sure that help would arrive? And what's holding up these rescues? The altitude? Money? I don't understand.

I think of Ludo and my heart softens: he must be in a terrible state of despair too. And my Jean-Jean! Don't worry, my love; it's going to be OK.

A flood of thoughts crosses my mind; a current of chills runs down my back. I'm drained, spaced out by fatigue. I have to lie down. I remember that I have my sponsors' banners in the outside pocket of my suit. I grab them to insulate myself. First I lay my pole on the layer of snow, then I spread the banners on top. While sitting, I have pins and needles, frozen buttocks and a wrecked back from the contractions and the stooped position that the cramped space forces me to fit into. I need to relax my back and my legs. I rotate gently so as not to scratch the ceiling and knock the stalactites. I position my head on the exit side, my feet at the bottom of the ramp, my back to the depths and in front of the snowy wall with its fine concretions, delicately deposited by the wind. The mountain has this ability to naturally shape artistic works and remodel them over the course of time.

I shiver for more than two hours, maybe three, maybe four. I'm shaken by long and severe chills at regular intervals. Then they stop and I feel like my body has finally stopped fighting against the cold. I don't know how it's possible, but I manage to stop shivering and I feel pretty good. The temperatures are polar outside. In here, I don't know and I prefer not to know. I push myself up on my hands and initiate a 180-degree rotation. My knees follow the movement while staying in place on the ground. And I end up leaning on my opposite side. I curl my knees up close to my body, in a foetal position, so as not to lose heat. This change of side eases my circulation, which was constricted on my right side; but the left side is quickly frozen and the cold diffuses across my whole body. The chill grasps me tight in its stranglehold. I position my back against the wall of snow as though the wall of ice could warm me up, wrap me in its arms, defend me from the cold which harasses me without mercy.

The fluttering snow, shorn off and blown up from the depths of the glacier, is so cold, so fine, that it infiltrates everywhere, chilling me a little more. But it also keeps me from falling asleep, which leaves me torn. I am exhausted. My body is fighting to warm me up, my head to stop me sleeping. The wind rushes across my eyes and sprinkles me with flakes of snow. It freezes my neck. I am attacked from all sides, caught between two cold masses: one rising from the depths of the glacier, blowing with all its harsh icy coldness; the other Siberian, descending from Nanga and racing into the numerous leaks in my roof. I'm shivering. The chills go up my spine, stronger and stronger, faster and faster, more and more violent. I don't want to sleep, and I can't, fortunately. I'm shattered. I long to rest, to take a break with a little nap. The night is extremely windy. I'm worried about Tom higher up. It's so harsh here.

I fight against the cold. I fight against my dark thoughts. The cold keeps me awake, but I'm shaking like a leaf. My mind wanders to Jean-Christophe. I think about him intensely.

I had to fall asleep. I'm no longer shivering. My body has relaxed. I dreamt of warmth, of hot tea, of an old lady who brought it to me and asked me for my shoes in exchange.

I rise, sit up. Once again, my head hits the ceiling: a freezing snow shower. I'm suffering. The unwelcome dream warmed me up, but it also sucked me towards an abyss of illusions from which I haven't really emerged. My feet are very cold, meaning I'm still alive. The aluminium foil wrapped around each foot on the morning of the 25th has been bothering me for over forty-eight hours and creates a cold sensation instead of insulating my feet. I need to remove it. I'm half asleep, immersed in this dream that's haunting me. Who is this old lady? I feel as though I know her. Her face reminds me of an advertising campaign on yoghurt pots, but also of a face in a Vermeer painting that we studied in a visual arts course at college. I make a superhuman effort and remove the aluminium layer from one foot. I put my socks back on; my boot is frozen, icy. I take it off – I'm better off, less cold, without it. I put it aside. I can't get the other boot off to remove the foil. I lie down. I fall asleep again, then wake up once more due to the snow freezing my face. I busy myself trying to clear it away as quickly as possible. Outside, the wind blows in gusts which lift up snow and pour white rain on my head, sticking together in an icy mask as the night goes by.

Daydream, extreme fatigue, exhaustion: this also happened to me during an adventure race in the World Championships in 2012. At the time, as part of Team Lafuma, we were in the middle of a series of French, European and world competitions. On this day, we had completed 120 hours of non-stop racing. I moved forward while dreaming and talking, but my brain was switched off. I was on a zip line and I asked my teammates: how do we do this with our bikes? A bizarre dream! They had woken me up while joking about it. But everyone then went on to experience the same thing at one point or another: a phase of REM sleep where the brain – tired and sleep-deprived for too long – dreams while the body is moving, advancing.

The race taught me a lot about managing effort, about the ability of the body and the brain to cope.

When I lift my head to the sky, I can see the stars through the chequerboard of ice carved by the wind. The crevasse reflects back at me in the depths of this great cold. The mirror of life, of my life. I feel like I've slept here before, as though I've already been awake here. This thought soothes me. The purity of the night protects me; the snow wraps me in its white sheet. My mind slips into the depths of the crevasse.

I went far away that night. In a world of dreams, to find Tom. I could have escaped from this world with him. But that was not my destiny. Shortly after my return, a shrink I was talking to – with floods of tears streaming down my cheeks, unable to close the floodgates – said to me:

'You saw your own death that night. And you saw Tom's with your own eyes the day before. Don't apologise for being alive, Élisabeth. Don't apologise for having survived. Tomek would never have wanted you to condemn yourself for him.'

Months later, I still can't get over it. I remain locked in a maze of unanswered questions, with days when I curse myself, when I am totally disorientated, devoid of anything. Incapable of thinking about the future, endlessly dwelling on the past. Time is frozen and no longer stretches; it sucks me into a vacuum and I no longer want to do anything. Time is only suffering. My anger replays on loop. Like the water in a mountain stream, my memories erode me, wear me down.

It took a year for the vice to loosen little by little, for me to start sleeping, climbing, cycling and running again without constantly revisiting the same images or reliving the same despair.

# 27 JANUARY 2018, 3 OR 4 A.M.

———————

I wake up with a jolt. My foot! My boot! I'm in socks! My left boot is no longer next to me on my little snow ledge. It must have fallen to the bottom of the crevasse. How can I recover it? I can't see anything – my head torch batteries are dead. I am so useless! I fell asleep; I must have moved and knocked it to the bottom of this freezer blasting icy air. I want to pee, but I'm lying on a thin snow bridge at the edge of the abyss. The limited space prevents me from taking off my suit. I move to the exit of the crevasse, the only place that's less cramped. I undo my suit and try to stabilise myself while squatting, but remain unbalanced so as not to place my left foot on the ice. I press my hands on the outer lip of the crevasse. In one way or another, I pee. I sprinkle my sock, I curse. Then I carefully put all my clothes back on.

I place my foot at the bottom of my suit to protect it. I curl up like a child, fearing that the night will pummel me again in the icy shroud of the crevasse. I can't wait for this night to end, to get out of this frozen hell.

My sock is wet and the suit quickly slips; my foot remains in the air. But I am too exhausted to react.

I switch on the inReach. I find several messages from Ludo:

At 2 a.m.:

*If you read these words force yourself to reply.*
*Don't let yourself get cold. Hold on.*[49]

3.32 a.m.:

*Urubko is part of the rescue team. 6 people. 2 helis.*[50]

I prefer not to reply; I have to save my fingers. I hope for dawn. I doze. All of a sudden, I find myself in my childhood bedroom in my parents' house. Each evening, my eyes were fixed on Everest – on the poster above my bed of the South-West Face, at least. Below, there was a verse from the Bible: 'I will lie down and sleep in peace, for you alone, O Lord, make me dwell in safety.' A comforting verse for me, as a child who was always afraid of the dark. I was amazed by the world above. I often asked my parents how mountaineers climbed to the heights of the eternal snow. They responded: you'll find out when you grow up!

We often went hiking in the mountains. I was four years old when my parents took us to the Glacier Blanc refuge in the Briançonnais, in the heart of the Écrins. My brother – who is two years older – and I climbed on our own, like grown-ups, without batting an eyelid. I always wanted to go higher. At home, I spent my time perched high in the lime tree with my brother, or in the trees on the edge of the Lozière, the little neighbouring stream. I dreamt of mountains, scanned IGN and mountaineering books, gazed at photos.[51] The world above intrigued me more and more, like a taboo challenge, a whisper of the unknown. I wanted to explore these ridges, to draw my own pictures. This was in reality where my life as a mountaineer and my expeditions started – there in my daydreams, my imagination, my aspirations. I can no longer explain how I came to be on Nanga this winter, but it was during these childhood years that everything started.

At the age of thirteen, I worked in the fields with my brother during the summer holidays. It was ten kilometres from home. I wasn't old enough to work legally, but I wanted to experience life first-hand and earn a bit of money 'by the sweat of my brow'.

We were the youngest workers, but also among the fastest, the most serious. My parents told us over and over: 'When you do something, do it well.' In the middle of the season, our bosses asked us to stay on and even promoted us! We were responsible for grading the garlic and then detasselling the corn. We went to work on our bikes. In the evenings, rather than taking the direct route, we preferred to follow a small mountain bike trail, just to fill our lungs with air. I worked like this in the fields every summer until the age of twenty. I then went on to pick apricots, which took me away from dusty fields and spared my back!

Alongside gymnastics competitions, every weekend I hiked with my parents in the Écrins, Queyras, Vercors or Dévoluy. We sometimes left at 3 a.m. There, I was immersed in contemplation and wonder in the face of the resplendent, ever-changing natural world; playing with my brother, laughing at everything and nothing, in the innocence of our youth. I always asked for more; I was never tired. The steeper it was, the more I liked it. The higher it was, the more it fascinated me.

On Sundays we went to pray in church with my mum. We were believers and churchgoers. Just before I was born, my mother learnt that she had cancer. I was two months old when she started intensive radiation therapy. My dad worked and also had to take care of my brother, who was then just two years old. Throughout my entire first year of life, I was looked after by my aunt.

Informed and influenced by two of her brothers – Amédée, who worked at the Pasteur Institute in Paris and had eliminated all processed food from his diet; and François, who cultivated and ate organic food – my mother adopted instinctotherapy during her illness, then the practice of eating raw food, alternating between monodiets of fruit and vegetables. It was a traumatic period, but after a year, the cancer was in remission. On the recommendation of naturopaths, my parents then started hiking. We spent all our summers in Puy Aillaud, a hamlet in the High Alps near Vallouise and Pelvoux, and that's where my love of nature and physical exertion is rooted. It was there too that I discovered the smells of fodder, the flowering meadows of gentians, the high-altitude lakes, the panorama of peaks, the Écrins massif – so many beauties and pleasures I've never tired of and revisit whenever I can.

My mother's cancer and her treatment also had an impact on our eating habits. We ate organic food at home, which at the time was unusual and led to a mismatch with our daily lives, whether at school for us or in a professional context for my parents.

We had a garden to supply us with vegetables, a goat for milk and cheese, and chickens and rabbits. Our diet was very healthy. My parents always said: 'You are what you eat.' With each passing day, I get a sense of the extent to which everything they passed on to me – simple and healthy fundamentals – helps me in my adult life.

I can no longer thank my mum for that. She died on 27 August 1995 from a second cancer. Less than a year after her diagnosis, eaten away by illness, she left us. It was an awful time in my life.

8.38 a.m. New message from Ludo:

*Give update pls rescuers setting off. Good luck sis.*[52]

8.53 a.m. I respond to him:

*5 toes frozen on left foot it's like wood. I must see cauchy*[53] *urgently.*[54]

Ludo:

*What do you have with you?*[55]

*Nothing.*[56]

9 a.m. Ludo:

*I'm organising that with Cauchy. We're all with you.*[57]

9.57 a.m. Ludo:

*help is on its way. hold on.*[58]

10.08 a.m. Ludo:

*rescuers have already collected rescue team from K2.*

*Waiting on visibility for take-off towards nanga.*[59]

The sun kisses the edge of the crevasse. I decide to come out of my hole. First, I need to recover my boot. I descend the snow cone. I downclimb a narrow ice gully for three metres, arms in opposition on the white wall. With my right crampon, I cut steps so I can put my foot back in my sock. But I can't see anything: my boot must have reached the bottomless depths of the crevasse. I give up and go back up.

I wait. I'm cold, I'm thirsty and yet I only have to stick out my tongue to drink particles of frozen water from all around my face. My face is frosted, my eyelids glazed, my throat dry and on fire. I remove some ice crystals which are obstructing my vision from my lashes. This crevasse is too hostile; I dream of the sun. There must be a solution! Get moving instead of suffering! I have to try again, go further down into the crevasse, search, explore. I descend, concentrate. I reach a build-up of snow and hesitate to move forward, as the terrain doesn't fill me with confidence. But after a few metres, I see my boot, planted in the snow by the front point of the crampon. I dig steps to it, grab it. A yawning hole looms before me. How lucky that my crampon planted this way! I go back into the ice cone. On the snowy ledge, I empty the snow that fills my boot and put it on. Crampons on feet, I'm getting out of this freezer. I am finally outside! I lie on the terrace and let the relative heat invade my body as the sun caresses my face. A moment of comfort, the first since I plunged into freezing hell.

I'm incredibly thirsty. I need to hydrate. I haven't had anything to drink for two nights and three days. I haven't eaten either, but I've forgotten about hunger; only thirst manifests itself. I have to remedy it: at this altitude, you have to drink at least a litre and a half of water per day to combat the effects of dehydration. I don't know how my body has managed to overcome the freezing temperatures with a lack of water and energy. My body is walking a fine line, right at the end of my tether, I know, but my will to get out of this situation seems to increase my strength tenfold. What keeps me holding on mentally, during these hours of waiting, is the hope of rescue, the exchanges with Ludo providing little glimmers of life. I know that retreat lower down on this route is impossible. I save my energy in case I have to go back up, keeping this option in my head as a last resort. I endure the wait for the unfolding rescues calmly, drawing relaxation from an unknown source. The sun heals my wounds, soothes me.

The snow and the ice around me represent a significant quantity of water, but I can only absorb a minuscule amount. The ice hurts my mouth, sticking to my tongue or my palate because of the extreme cold. When it's too cold, I have to remove the ice cube stuck to my mucous membranes. In doing so, I tear off a piece of skin, flesh, or tongue. It's painful. Rehydrating with snow is difficult: I feel like I'm only making my frozen gloves even wetter by collecting ice, while hurting my mouth and lips.

> When I got home, I realised that communicating solely with Ludo had been the best solution. He succeeded in finding the right words, when psychologically I was ready to crack under the weight of desperation or despondency, or on the verge of venting my anger.
>
> If I'm here today, it's because he managed this rescue masterfully.
>
> If I had communicated too much with Jean-Christophe, the emotion would have overwhelmed me, upset me, caused me to sink.

10.30 a.m. Ludo:

*harness on? double-locking karabiner? everything is ready they're waiting for visibility on their side*[60]

I immediately respond:

*But the visibility is good!!!*[61]

I don't understand.

10.48 a.m. Ludo:

*still waiting on visibility*[62]

*yan[63] forecasts fog at 3 p.m. but clear night, so it should clear up*[64]

My gaze still wanders back to the glacier above me, where Tomek is lying. I'm so scared for him. The polar wind sweeps across my face, taking my prayers to him.

I still don't understand the situation. I interrogate myself about this decision that was imposed on me, telling me that I should descend so the helicopters could rescue Tomek. I see with a shudder of fear that the sky is darkening and the weather deteriorating quickly at the altitude at which Tomek is stranded. My eyes remain fixated for an eternity on the clouds sweeping faster and faster across the plateau. I am dismayed, powerless. My throat tightens. I can't digest the truth, the reality that I'm living through. I feel awfully responsible, guilty. Why did I listen to Ludo and the rescue team? I should be with Tomek just now; I should be helping him, protecting him.

The cruelty of it all overwhelms me.

We mobilised all our thoughts, all our energy, all our strength and resources to try to survive the inhumane cold of the first night. Then I believed that outside help could save Tomek and snatch him back from his tragic fate, by getting him out of this trap. What a presumption!

The memory of what we have experienced in recent days assails me, torments me, weighs me down. And the terrible events of the past two nights and the last day are replaying on loop in my head. The image of Tomek's face, traumatised by the cold, crushes me. This lonely place is simultaneously devastating and comforting. I'm safe on my ledge, but resigned, tired and weakened by all this time waiting at high altitude. I'm cold and I can't get warm, between the lack of food, the wind, exhaustion and thirst. I spend the day hoping hour after hour. Physical as well as mental fatigue engulfs me. I'm not thinking of anything; I just want to have some peace, warmth, to get out of here. Exhausted, I long to fall asleep and wake to the sound of the rotors. Save Tom up there and then pick me up. My God, we need help! A rope! Some equipment to protect us from the cold. This hope keeps me in suspense and occupies my mind, but it is in vain, I gradually realise.

I'm terribly thirsty.

11.53 a.m. Ludo:

*we're pushing for take-off but we're not in control. Is it windy?*[65]

11.57 a.m. Éli:

*wind perfect but not much time before cloud*[66]

12.06 a.m. Ludo:

*we're pushing, we're pushing, they're going to leave*[67]
*we're on it hold on sis. We're not leaving you we're looking into*
*everything.*[68]

How could I have exposed myself to so many risks with Tom? All the
safety protocols we had devised collapsed like houses of cards! In my
head, I keep going over the chain of events which derailed everything.
I am tortured by the nagging question of my responsibility towards
Tom, to his wife, to his children, to Jean-Christophe, to my family.
My controlled life has escaped me. Why all these risks? Why did we
expose ourselves like this? Why go up there and keep returning? This
question that I'm often asked today, here I'm the one screaming it.
What are Tom and I still doing here this year? Were we clinging on to
a past aspiration, which has now been realised? Did we return to fulfil
our dream of a winter ascent on this mountain?

For Tomek, it's clear: this year, he wanted revenge on the 'failure' of
2016, a balm for the wound of his 'stolen' summit, for the humiliating
and hurtful criticism he'd been subjected to. Tomek doesn't give
credence to the first winter ascent in 2016; he remains obsessed with
seeking evidence of this non-summit. Yet I told him that he was
making my head spin with this obsession and that he should stop
going on about his bitterness. This year, he came to get 'his' first, even
wanting to climb to the summit in winter in pure alpine style and via
the Buhl route, the route opened by the Austrian Hermann Buhl in
the summer of 1953. A crazy challenge in winter, to my mind: the
exposure to the wind is too strong there. In 2015, Tomek and I had
arrived at the foot of the final Buhl ridge. At the time, I didn't know
the ascent conditions beyond 7,000 metres well, but I had descended
with the certainty that this route was very aesthetically appealing, but
far too exposed and too long to be tackled in winter.

I wanted to complete a traverse at 7,200 metres, connecting the
Diama glacier to the Bazhin Hollow and finishing modestly by the

summit pyramid of the classic ascent route, the Kinshofer, the first ascent of which was made in summer 1962 by an Austrian team.

So we planned to install our last shared camp at between 7,200 and 7,400 metres, then to separate and each set off on our respective route. But that didn't suit me: it was too unrealistic, too risky!

If Tomek had followed the Buhl route alone, things could quickly have gone wrong. He'd been fantasising about that route since 2015. He was confident; whereas I found his project disproportionate, over the top. So what did he want to prove to the world? In winter 2013, Tomek spent twenty-one nights alone on this mountain. I don't think anyone else has stayed so long at an altitude of 7,200 metres in the middle of Himalayan winter! Tomek is a force of nature; he is very strong, physically and mentally, to the point of seeming invincible to me, of an unyielding resistance. So, why the need to embark on the Buhl route? Finally, I convinced him to take the Diamir route and we decided to go to the summit together. Our team bond was restructured on this simpler, more cohesive project: climb together, reach the summit and descend together.

And me? What did I come in search of here once again? What is certain is that I didn't come to get the first winter ascent. That has been achieved and it's all the better for it, since I was able to return to Nanga in peace, without pressure. The 2016 expedition knocked me off balance: I felt committed to a race against my will, to a rivalry that was beyond me, and I found the tensions difficult to digest on the mountain or at Base Camp. Ultimately, not getting to the summit that year was the best thing that could have happened to me, allowing me to refocus on my personal and primary objective: to climb Nanga in winter, in alpine style, by my own means.

I regret the way in which Tom's history with Simone Moro played out: the controversy, the hurtful words exchanged, the low blows that made me question my outlook on the mountaineering sphere, disappointing me and driving me away.

So, what did I really want? To finish my project, to answer all my questions about the capacity of the body and mind above 8,000 metres in winter? Yes. But also to listen to the little voice inside telling me I'd always regret it if I didn't finish this project? Yes. Returning meant putting myself in the right place and, in January 2018, I only wanted to be on an 8,000-metre peak in winter and nowhere else!

In short, this year my objective was to climb the mountain following my own path, my motivation, in line with the guiding principles I'd held since my early years. Competing with my desires, my rules, rather than seeking firsts and records. Without necessarily giving up on performance, but following my own perceptions and aspirations at that point.

I scan the sky. It's half past twelve. Why isn't help arriving?

And why did I need to come back a fourth time – one time too many? – to this peak? Why do these high summits, which can be so hostile, hold such an attraction for me?

In the months and years following my mother's death, the mountains have been my refuge. In the absence of maternal love, I have found peace in the green shoots of nature or in the whiteness of eternal snow, close to the sun's rays, to the sky! For me, my father and my brother, this was our piece of heaven. I recall a letter left to my mum by her father: 'Remember this well, my child: if ever you are grieving, go to the forest and walk with your eyes wide open to look at the world around you. Because in each tree, in each bush, in each animal, in each flower, you will find divine presence and power. Through this, you will be comforted and you will forget your torments.'

In 2009, I came back from Annapurna alone after desperately searching for Martin Minařík, my Czech climbing companion, in a snowstorm for hours on end. On my return, I stopped everything. I didn't want to hear talk of mountains any more. I had suffered too much. I had too many questions inside me and not a single answer. I no longer wanted to be responsible for someone. I didn't want to decide any more. I was suffocating; I kept telling myself that we should have turned around before, that we had continued too far, etc. But who is responsible? There were two of us up there to decide, two to evaluate the risk, to measure it, two to know one another perfectly at altitude, two adults responsible for our actions towards our loved ones, and two to bear the consequences. But I descended alone.

For four years, I stopped going on expeditions and I threw myself head-first into adventure racing. It was an intense period, enabling me to understand and forget about Annapurna, to take stock of this flame that attracted me to the Himalaya; but also to discover a new environment, a new activity, a joyful life with my teammates in Team Lafuma.

But a life without mountains, without high altitude, is as unimaginable for me as life without my husband.

Up there, I feel at home; I live singular, magical experiences that are complex to describe and share on my return. What I experience arises from a mysterious alchemy which I find difficult to put into words. For example, when I found myself alone at the top of Pequeño Alpamayo in Bolivia in 2006 or on Lhotse in Nepal in 2017, the emotion that took hold of me was mystifying: I was above the world, alone and in harmony with nature. My gaze settled on prestigious summits that I'd dreamt of for years. I shouted with joy into the wind; I sent thanks to the heavens for these unique moments of intensity and happiness. Nothing else mattered any more, just the pleasure which permeated every fibre in my body. These two climbs remain unique for me, as the crowning glory of my personal quest.

In Bolivia in 2006, I surpassed the height of Mont Blanc for the first time and climbed my first 5,000-metre peak. On Lhotse in spring 2017, I finally went beyond an altitude of 8,500 metres, and this was like a climax in my life: years of dreams, my love for heights, finally consecrated in a delightful harmony. It's part of what keeps me alive and makes me come alive, part of what fascinates me about life: the beauty of nature and of the world. I was alone on the summit, but also supported by loved ones from my past and present life.

In 2008, during my second trip to the Himalaya, I discovered the land of thin air on the Baltoro glacier in Pakistan. I surpassed the symbolic altitude of 8,000 metres among the highest peaks on Earth – every mountaineer's dream. I climbed the impossible mountains of my childhood. Since then, my heart has remained magnetised by these very high peaks where I lived magical moments, attaining a joy and contemplative state that is difficult to describe and share. My body adapts well to this environment: from the summit of Gasherbrum I, for example, I called my husband. He thought I had already returned to Base Camp because I was talking so normally, with my usual fast and jerky cadence, as though the lack of oxygen wasn't bothering me!

I have often been criticised for recounting my ascents too simply. My mountain stories have sometimes surprised people due to their 'no-nonsense' aspect which doesn't position me as a superwoman. I distance myself from the stories of adventurers with superhuman capabilities, the image projected since the beginning of Himalayan mountaineering. In short, I'm at odds with the narrative of 'mountaineering stars'. But in reality, most of these epic tales don't match up with what I've experienced at 8,000 metres. It's true that my body adapts rather quickly to new environments; I'm lucky to feel in my element at altitude. What I call modesty is considered a provocation.

But I don't let this bother me. I quickly came to understand the discrepancy between what I am and what the media expect of a Himalayan mountaineer: sensationalism, drama, records, superhuman mentality and physique … I don't belong in this show. I prefer reality.

Mountaineering allows me, I'm certain of it, to live better in society. For me, life down below is sometimes a burden. The stance I take is perhaps asocial or antisocial. In any case, the puffs of oxygen I get in the mountains cushion my daily connection with the world. They're my point of equilibrium. The escape from everyday life. The escape from social norms, from comfortable furnishings and a daily routine, which would place too many limits on my physical and spiritual aspirations and my desire for freedom. And the desire to live my own experiences, to make up my own mind.

I find myself fleeing ever further from a society that would like to decide for me. I know that the answers are inside me. I go up there to live authentically. When you know that the risks exist, when you face them, you live intensely and descend with an even greater love of life. On an expedition, my life is intensified, incandescent, much more intense than in any moment down below!

At altitude, I'm not trying to 'dance with death', as the saying goes. I don't go up there for the danger; my first objective remains always to get back down and not take risks. I go there to find life's pleasure, to head into the unknown, where my eyes sparkle, where I feel completely myself.

A message from Ludo draws me back from my long daydream. 1.03 p.m.:

> the helis have taken off, they have to refuel in the middle. We try
> a 3rd heli too in case as a relay[69]
> wind fog situation, hold on[70]

Hold on. Yes. Keep hope alive. But I'm really angry with myself.

Why return to Nanga Parbat four times, having promised never to throw myself at the same summit twice in desperation? Of course, it's a mountain whose history has always fascinated me. I studied it for a long time, dissected its routes. I read all the accounts of ascents, looked at all the available images; my imagination wandered for many years around the flanks of this icy giant.

But to tell the truth, this year, I didn't particularly want to return to Nanga. After three expeditions in a row on the mountain, I wanted to have a chance to breathe, to attempt another summit and experience the pleasure of discovery once again.

Following my first expedition here in 2013 with Daniele Nardi, I had returned fascinated by winter in the Himalaya, the isolation of this mountain, the management and adaptation that such a project requires; but also certain that the ascent was possible and that I would come back. Nanga Parbat is magnificent in winter: solidified, draped with blue sections of sheer ice, frozen by time and the cold, while winds dance around the peaks.

Two years later, in 2015, I remained immersed in the solitude of Nanga for more than a week and was confronted with everything a winter ascent of an 8,000-metre peak in Pakistan entails: conditions much more severe than in Nepal, sometimes an apocalyptic mix of biting cold, raging wind and extreme temperatures. But it is precisely this dimension – survival in a hostile environment – which intrigued me, fascinated me. On these climbs, which required a mixture of endurance, courage, motivation and willpower, I drew great confidence from within and piqued my curiosity. Nanga also taught me about humility, risk management, human limits and, above all, about giving up. I descended with even more dreams than on the way up, certain that I wanted to return.

In 2016, I had a less positive experience on the expedition: too many people, too much rivalry. Fifteen days waiting in Chilas to obtain all the permits and do the paperwork, and we missed the only possible weather window in January. We were disappointed, Tomek and I both, despite all the energy and passion that we had demonstrated.

1.53 p.m. Ludo:

*just in case, Alex has left food at 6,000m behind the ridge down and to right … last resort*[71]
*still two hours before arrival of helis.*[72]

But why is it taking so long? Why all these never-ending delays?

2.07 p.m. I respond to Ludo:

*2 hrs? are they coming from Islamabad?*[73]

I can quickly become ironic when responding to life events that are beyond my control. I pull myself together:

*I can try to descend a bit! but little energy left[74]*
*reaching summit at night is ultimately costing us dear besides our*
*happiness[75]*
Ludo:
*stay on possible landing zone for the moment. I'll tell you if you*
*need to descend[76]*

Why come back this year? Why did we both return to Nanga? Were we climbing in search of an ideal?

Tom and I were tired of coming back to this mountain. Nothing – or very little – was still unknown. We examined the question from all sides. For us, the only thing missing was the summit. Was it important? The only positive answer I can offer is: 'Finish my 8,000-metre winter project, in alpine style; find answers to all the questions posed by this type of ascent, so that I never regret not having pursued my dream.' To be able to move on. Today, that seems ridiculous.

So, why go back? A winter ascent in the Himalaya on an 8,000-metre peak is the critical factor in my mountaineering life, driven by my stubbornness. The stories of Jean-Christophe Lafaille have always fascinated me: the necessary organisation, the management of complicated conditions, human ability and limits, difficult acclimatisation, short windows of opportunity, strategic climbing.[77] I really wanted to experience conditions other than in the classic seasons (spring, summer and autumn) in the troposphere. An 8,000-metre peak is an environment in which I feel good, where I can express myself differently. I no longer purged on routes, on summits, but on long journeys to the high mountains, on universes where I could test human limits. For 2018, I had lots of projects, including a major one in spring on Everest: the highest – but also the most expensive – peak in the world. Yet my budget was, as always, very tight. Since deciding to take a leave of absence from teaching in 2016 to devote myself entirely to mountaineering, I've lived from expedition to expedition thanks to my partners – Valandré, TeamWork, Everest Travaux

Acrobatiques, Grivel, Blue Ice. I have to divide the budget they offer me to the best of my ability, according to my objectives. However, an expedition in Nepal in winter costs twice as much as in spring and is three times more expensive than a winter expedition in Pakistan.

A winter ascent is more expensive at any rate given the low number of climbers; you can't share logistics like the permit or the liaison officer, nor the cost of the porters and cook. Moreover, in winter, the bet is always more risky because the weather often destroys a year of preparation: the chance of summiting reduces to only around twenty per cent. A winter expedition to Nepal would have ruined my spring project of climbing Everest. So, if I wanted to go on a winter ascent expedition, Nanga was the only option. But finding climbing companions, especially since the first ascent had already been done, was a lost cause. So I planned to go there alone.

Tom is broke. All the money he earns as a mechanic retouching old vehicles for a large company in Ireland is devoted to his children's education: Max and Tonia, the two eldest, who live with their mother Joana in Poland; and Zoïa, his youngest child, who lives with him and Anna in Ireland. Like me, for each expedition, he has to seek the necessary funding and he often resorts to crowdfunding. His 'fans' have supported him for years, showing the extent to which his unique ties with Nanga Parbat, which has become his mountain, inspires them. He had already tried to launch other projects, on Gasherbrums I and II and even Everest. In vain: only the funding campaigns for Nanga are successful. So the wheel turned full circle for him. 'Éli, I can find money, but only if it's for Nanga,' he had told me on the phone. However, his obsession had tired him; he'd had enough of this mountain. But everything was dragging him back again. As though his destiny was linked to it.

So the choice of summit was imposed on us this year.

My story resonates with Tom's, and his with mine. Our lives are so different, and yet I find in him the echo of my questions and my doubts. But I would rather bury my head in the sand than look at them too closely. Deep down, I no longer have my original motivation for Nanga, but that scares me. A shift from a passion for exploration to imprisonment? I'm aware of it, but I'm held captive.

When I have closed my eyes at home in the Drôme, I've escaped into the high peaks, to the Christmases spent up there on Nanga. And then I've had a gut feeling of desire, a sense of joy from reliving the difficult but magical moments, far away from everything! I felt that returning would mean being in the right place. This challenge of climbing Nanga in alpine style in winter has been my lifeblood.

3.24 p.m. Ludo:
*heli not very far how's it going?*[78]
3.47 p.m. Éli:
*it's ok super thirsty and hungry and 5mins sleep*[79]
3.50 p.m. Ludo:
*they'll arrive in 30 mins. Landing BC to drop team.*
*And to ascend light.*[80]
Ludo:
*Are you capable of catching a rope in flight and holding on well?*[81]
*With some knots [and] a dead weight? and a karabiner to clip*
*into … get ready with harness.*[82]
I reply to him:
*no or with karabiner I am burnt out.*[83]
Ludo:
*If it doesn't work he'll try to land or if not drop team.*[84]
5.02 p.m. Ludo once again:
*Confirm to us. Rescue ok? If slightest problem tell me we have a 3rd heli.*[85]
Well, no: I still hear nothing, I've had enough of waiting for these rescues that I've been promised for hours but which never arrive.
I respond:
*no, no rescue*[86]
5.11 p.m. Ludo:
*You can't see them?*[87]

Me:

   No[88]

5.14 p.m. Ludo:

   *Do you hear them? fog? they are there.*[89]

Me:

   *Nobody fog ok 3rd heli?*[90]

Ludo asks me if I hear them. I don't know. I don't believe so, I doubt it. About an hour ago, I returned to my makeshift shelter. The only 'rotors' I can hear are those of the raging wind on the Mazeno Ridge. The famous jet-engine noise of 8,000-metre peaks in winter. The sounds merge. No, it's not the heli; it's the gusts of wind which whistle in my ears. I don't want to hope in vain once again.

My inReach has almost no battery left. I have to save the precious three per cent that remains before it enters safety mode and triggers an emergency, because from then on, it will be impossible to send messages. I will therefore no longer be able to communicate. I send a message to Ludo to warn him of the inReach situation. I know he'll understand perfectly; he's experienced it himself in the mountains.

5.23 p.m.:

   *I'm going to die, soon no battery.*[91]

I can no longer bear this waiting in vain! I get the impression that these exchanges are useless, that they're all a decoy. I send this message out of despair: I want to make Ludo react! I no longer understand anything.

5.40 p.m. Ludo:

   *new rescue heli tomorrow. Rescue team climbing. 6,000m tent*
   *food ridge down right 10 min*[92]

The word 'tomorrow' slaps me in the face. The same as yesterday before the hell of the night. This word that sounds so bad to my ears. I can't live through another night of waiting! I have to descend. I have to take my destiny into my own hands. I have to get out of here and get off this mountain alone.

After all these hours of waiting, my slim hope turns to despair. I don't understand what's happening, what the Pakistani rescuers have planned. Why was I told to descend, to abandon Tomek, if they hadn't taken off, if they aren't arriving? I've been suffering the consequences for more than a day, eaten away by guilt, sapped by the cold. And Tomek is up there alone, so weakened.

I've been waiting here for twenty-four hours for the rescuers who were supposed to recover Tomek. I've followed all the instructions I was given. I've done everything I was told to do. Tomek can no longer move; the only thought that reassures me is that I know he is very strong and capable of resisting this terrible cold better than anyone. He's the gentleman of Nanga, who has spent countless nights up there. However, I'm struggling to ward off the terror which has gripped me since Tomek told me that he could no longer see.

Suddenly, everything changes again. Just like at the summit. I understand that there is no longer any hope of rescue here. And I feel deep inside that I have to move, keep on moving and go down. It's a vital emergency.

I can't spend hours waiting around doing nothing any more, no matter what Ludo or the Pakistani rescuers say. It's up to me to take up the reins, or I'll remain on this mountain forever.

It's forty-eight hours after our decision to continue to the summit, more than twenty-four hours since I agreed to descend, having decided to stay as close as possible to Tomek and thus to follow the Kinshofer route instead of our ascent route. Now I make the decision to continue alone and dive into the night, despite my frostbitten toes. I'm going to go down; I'm going to reach Base Camp tomorrow morning and I will come to Tom's rescue! Ludo is asking me not to move, to keep waiting, but I've been waiting in these inhuman conditions for two days! Two days during which Tomek has been at his worst, two days during which I've been suffering. I know, I feel that I have to flee from this mountain. My place is no longer here.

I no longer want to be that small vessel in the immensity of the ocean, tossed about by the waves and the wind, without a rudder, unable to control anything. I take over the helm. I am responsible for my situation and if we are in it, it's our fault. I should have understood that Tomek was in a bubble, obsessed by his communication with Fairy, depressed at Base Camp, isolated in his mystical quest, much more closed-off than in previous years.

I'm holding out hope; I'm going to find a solution to get down, to come to Tom's aid. I'm going to find resources, get down to Base Camp and, if things get tricky down below, get my arse into gear to downclimb and get out of this trap. And as for whether the fixed ropes continue or not … I have no choice; I have to go and explore!

I follow my instinct. I know the night will be long, but I'll be at Base Camp tomorrow. Yesterday's anxiety has vanished. The cruel forty-eight hours that I've just lived through, the traumatic images – Tomek's appalling state, his voice, his face, his hands – now act as fuel to get out of this forced wait, out of this trap, and to go and seek help for him. I have to try to escape this hell, this fatal confinement on the mountain. I have to move in order to live and to survive!

The plan is clear in my head, chasing away the ghosts and disillusions that tormented me during the night. I feel that no one will come to look for us; it's up to me to act if I want to live. I have to get off this mountain and organise a rescue down below for Tomek as quickly as possible. The wind is blowing stronger and stronger, sweeping accumulated snow from above the slopes of sheer ice. My direction is Base Camp; my priority is to move, to escape the hell of night-time, to go ahead and focus on what I have to do. Enduring another night outside without moving is out of the question. I sense that it would be fatal. I have to fight to survive, fight to get back to my husband. I can't abandon Jean-Christophe; I can't put him through that. I have to fight and get down from this mountain alive.

# 27 JANUARY 2018,
# 6 P.M.

---

I send a message to Ludo:

*I'll try to descend as far as there are ropes.*[93]

Then I switch off my inReach. It's 6 p.m. I will not see Ludo's response until much later:

*rescue team say don't move.*[94]

My first steps are hesitant and awkward. I don't know how to bear weight on my numb foot. I feel as though my toes have been replaced by a liquid mass, like they're detached from my body. I'm apprehensive about planting my foot. But, surprisingly, it doesn't hurt. I've no idea how long this will continue, but for the time being it's miraculous. I can use my foot; I can walk. On the other hand, shooting pains in my hands remind me that I'm far from being out of the woods.

I plunge into the darkness. I make some noise with my crampons to crush the weight of silence, of solitude, to drown out my doubts and fears. Will the rest be beyond me? Will I come to a dead end?

The slope is smooth, varnished, sustained at fifty to sixty degrees, with terribly hard ice. The depths of night obscure the route, and fortunately so! This way, I don't feel sucked into the void, drawn into the abyss. If I start sliding down this field of ice, it'll be over for me. I keep going, meticulously. I soon feel the tranquillity of the mountain and, paradoxically, the darkness brings a sense of security.

Everything seems improbable, unreal. I'm descending at night, without a head torch, on a route I don't know, without any equipment: no ice axe or belay device, no French prusik, no ice screws or dynamic rope.[95] Without having had a drink for fifty-five hours at least. Almost sleepless for eighty hours apart from my daydreams and last night's hallucinated torments. I cling with all my heart to some words my husband sent me during the climb to the summit a few days ago, like a talisman of caution in the face of the bad weather forecast:

*My darling, please, be at Base Camp on the 27th!*[96]

The pallid light of the moon is reflected on the Mummery Spur, as a nod to our experience in 2013, like a heaven-sent comfort. The Mazeno Ridge stands out majestically in the sky. The moon reflects the blue ice curtains of the Kinshofer route. I'm moving forward thanks to this fortuitous moon, after my head torch gave up the ghost. Fascinated by the relatively warm light that it gives me, I let myself slide along the ropes, forgetting for a moment the fragility and boldness of my undertaking. The question of what will happen below no longer surfaces. I just know that I have to descend through the night at my own pace. I take off my goggles because I can't see enough definition any more. A cold wind whips my face and freezes my corneas instantly. I protect my eyes with my glove while they adjust. I have to screw up my eyes to see more clearly.

My thoughts go round in circles: keep fingers warm—move toes— squint to protect my eyes. Keep fingers warm—move toes—squint to protect my eyes. Move forward.

I follow the ropes, like Ariadne's thread. These ropes that I normally run away from. How ironic! I've always avoided the fixed ropes installed from Base Camp to the summit. If I go up there, it's by my own means, full stop. Yet on normal routes, it's difficult to escape them these days. Fixed ropes attached to the mountain are replacing the ice axe. There is no dynamic rope between climbers, no ice screw on the harness, no French prusik. Just a hand jumar, a handle which you pull on to haul yourself up; and a belay device and a lanyard to descend. These ropes are carried on the backs of high-altitude porters, while the client carries only a light bag. I find this practice very far removed from the natural conditions of ascent and from genuine exploration of the high mountain environment. But tonight these ropes are saving my life, as well as alleviating my suffering.

How can they still be there and be accessible; why aren't they imprisoned in the ice? Nanga hasn't been climbed for three summers following the terrorist attack in 2013.[97]

The first climbers who returned in 2016 ascended almost entirely in alpine style. And in the last two years, few commercial expeditions have passed through here.

In any case, this lifeline seems to have unfolded for me and it reassures me. I stay focused, making sure I keep moving so as not to freeze on the spot.

> On my return, I will learn that I owe my salvation to a Korean commercial expedition from September 2017 whose climbers had placed these guiding lines for their clients, and also to the mild autumn weather which left the ropes free of ice.

The temperature drops gradually as the wind increases. It stings the top of my face. Fortunately, my nose and chin are protected by my hood. My fingers suffer acutely from the cold. I feel ice crystals form in the pulp of my knuckles.

Jean-Christophe's words keep ricocheting in my head:

*My darling, please, you have to be at Base Camp on 27 January. After that, a big atmospheric disturbance will arrive. Please, be down there on the 27th.*[98]

The weather is getting worse. I see filaments in the sky arriving from the Diamir Valley. I know the weather perfectly on this mountain and, over the course of my expeditions, I have learnt to read the signs of slight deterioration or disturbance. The sky above the mountains of Afghanistan's Hindu Kush is darkening, which means that a significant change is coming. I prefer to run towards life rather than wait for death to come to me, even though I don't stop to think about death and have never given it a thought until now.

I lift my eyes to the plateau. Visibility is non-existent. A front of lenticular clouds runs from east to west. I know Tom is sheltered, but what condition is he in now? An unanswered, nagging question which has been haunting me since I left him over twenty-four hours ago.

I have never known such complete solitude, but paradoxically, I draw great strength from this ordeal. I surprise myself by advancing in this new night with a sense of calm. I no longer feel particular emotions: no more anger, no more incomprehension. I have a goal and I'm moving forward.

To quench my thirst, I prise off pieces of ice, but these instantly sticks to my lips, to my tongue, my palate; they don't melt! My mouth is bloody, my skin ripped off, and I get thirstier and thirstier.

I function on autopilot, a bit like when I started the descent with Tom from the summit to the crevasse, except that this time, I'm forcing these automatic gestures on myself. I've left almost all of my equipment with Tomek to keep him secure and comforted in his shelter: my thick gloves, my ice axes, my karabiners. The only way to get down safely is to make the best use of what I have left: the leashes of my ice axes and a screwgate karabiner.[99] I use the leash as a French prusik to slow down the descent on the rope and lock in the event of a fall.

I take off my bulky overmittens for practical handiwork. On my screwgate karabiner, I tie an Italian hitch using the slack in the rope here. When the rope is too tight and I can't even tie a knot, I make a round turn on the karabiner. And in the worst-case scenario – which unfortunately happens frequently – when I have no slack, I just clip the karabiner on to the rope. But I always descend with two points connecting me to the fixed rope. I always screw my karabiner shut, checking the lock with my thumb before each departure.

I repeat these tasks in autopilot mode, dozens and dozens of times. I progress slowly; it's long, tedious. Around me, there's nothing but blue, a wall of sheer ice. I actually find myself in the ice field that I'd spotted from below, when it was shining in the dark and I swore I would never set foot there ...

My mind is completely focused on each of my movements. The end of my injured foot feels oddly like liquid. But I have faith in my steps, faith in my body. This body that I have worked hard all my life can't give up on me! I have shaped it, forged it, toughened it and placed it under duress for years, and today it has to deliver.

I enter a mixed zone of jumbled rock and ice. I descend automatically from belay to belay, focused on the action. Eat snow, blow warm air on to my hands from my mouth, handle the rope (French prusik—round turn—Italian hitch), screw up my karabiners, check, grab the rope, concentrate, suppress my fatigue, don't think about my fingers. And ask: what do I do if I get stuck? Climb back up? Stay at the end of the rope? Wait? No, it's too cold; it'll mean certain death. If I get stuck, I'll have to go back up and traverse at 7,200 metres; it's the only solution. But will I have enough strength and enough time before the weather disturbance arrives? It's pointless to procrastinate: keep going and find out! I continue for forty metres. I thank the unknown rope-fixers.

I miss my ice axes terribly! They are crucial tools in the mountains and usually I take care of them as I would a prized possession. Why did I leave them up there; why didn't I bring at least one? When I built the belay to secure Tom, I never thought I would need them for the next part, reaching Camp 3. But beyond that, it's madness. Without the providential fixed ropes, I would be incapable of going down. What a fool I am! Leaving my two tools up there could result in my demise further down the line. When I placed them, it was to ensure that Tomek wouldn't fall, wouldn't slip. But I'm cursing myself at this moment. As in many others.

Then I calm myself down because even with my ice axes, on this sheer, hard, blue ice, tilted at fifty degrees, it would be impossible for me to downclimb such a big drop. In any case, it would require an abseil rope. If I should slip, even my ice axes would not be able to arrest my fall on this icy slope. The ropes are my only lifeline!

It's a long and tedious battle, but also a step towards Base Camp, towards life. Jean-Christophe must be so worried!

I look up, to where Tomek is waiting for me. I know that I have a role to play in coming to his aid, but a long path extends and dips vertiginously towards our Base Camp. I am engaged in a new, vital race against the clock, and I have to win the game before the storm.

We believed that the challenge was to reach the summit by our own route. Yet the real challenge was to get back down from this mountain, from this hostile place. In the midst of my confused thoughts and the haze that surrounds me, I have to keep hold of my sense of reality. I helped Tomek to hang on to life for long hours.

I resume my descent. I advance without haste, in a methodical way. I'm walking on glass; the points of my crampons barely bite into this blue ice. I can clearly see my legs and my toes anchored in the ice, embedded, penetrating the film of glassy ice to bite on to the wall and secure my step. As though I have eyes at foot-level to dig into this pressure point. I occasionally slip with a screech that breaks the silence. Immediately, my hands grasp the rope firmly in reflex; I clench my teeth. But I descend and slide along this life-saving nylon thread.

I progress in a silent world. No noise from séracs or avalanches. I advance on the front points of my crampons, facing this slope of ice, facing the summit, facing Tomek, heading back to the void, back to Base Camp. I force myself to increase the pressure on the rope with my hands. I hold on tight despite the pain in my fingertips. A capsule of ice inside my glove now covers every last phalanx. I don't have emergency gloves any more. I left everything for Tomek. If he had brought at least one spare pair of gloves, I would not be here, freezing my hands! In this moment, his marginal approach exasperates me.

Each switch between ropes is a small victory over sleepiness, fatigue, exhaustion, thirst, cold. Time flies and I fight against it, to reach Camp 2, to find a shelter, and then descend to Base Camp. I disconnect myself from my hands, so that the damage, the pain, doesn't dominate my thoughts. My goal is down below. Here, it's death. I don't have a choice! Move! The cold is freezing.

> In retrospect, I understand that at this moment, there was only a very small chance of saving Tom. I was not aware of the extreme seriousness of his condition, the near-death state that I had all the same perceived in his face before leaving him, and my own brush with death the night before.
>
> Fortunately so, otherwise I might not have been able to move on. The brain is sometimes protective and survival instinct is a mysterious phenomenon.
>
> During these terrible days, I always thought about life for Tomek and me, and never about death for either of us. I never gave up hope of bringing Tom back to life, of succeeding in descending to Base Camp. Deep inside me, a positive energy projected me forward, protected me. Today, I wonder what this external or internal force is, the force which came to chase away the demons of the night, gave me the energy to survive, and tore me away from the trap that was closing in on me.

I'm thirsty. I grab some snow but it's too fine, light; in my mouth, it's no more than a drop. And my gloves get wetter in the process.

Over the course of the night, the wind gets stronger. Blizzards and winds enter the arena in an already freezing night. The clouds veil the mountains. Bad weather is coming. The wind lifts swirls of snow. This cold pierces my body, my bones, my flesh. I make an effort to move to warm myself up. I have reached the end of this little ice wall; it's miraculous that, apart from a mere five metres, these fixed ropes were not trapped in the ice.

I need to sit down for a bit on the rocks. I am tired and sleepiness is overtaking me. I set myself down. My eyes close, tyrannised by the cold and the wind and assaulted by fatigue. I need to rest my body a little to be able to set off again, to survive. I don't stop for very long. My position is very uncomfortable; the gusts of wind are too powerful and I can't switch off for even a few minutes. It's as if someone were pushing me down, telling me, 'Now is not the time to sit down here; go on, go, go down, you have nothing more to do here!' I feel like I'm falling, slipping, and I have to get back up. I am chilled to the bone in minutes. I'm dozing, but suddenly a violent icy slap of sleet wakes me up, puts me back on track. My hands hurt terribly. The pain is sometimes so sharp that it forces me to stop. With my forehead pressed against the ice, I snuggle my hands under my armpits, trying to warm up. I wait until the pain subsides. Then I set off again.

The weather is changing; I mustn't hang around. If I stop for too long, it will make things more difficult. I must keep moving all night long in order to survive. Get down off this mountain. Get myself out of this hell. My brain is programmed and it won't give up. All of these years spent training physically, forging a mind of steel, are now paying off.

I wander under the pallid moonlight that reveals fields of bright blue ice. I focus on my foot placement; I don't want to slip and have to grip the ropes harder between my traumatised hands. I force myself to mobilise as much as possible, contracting my hands to bring some blood to my extremities.

The slope has straightened and plunges into the Diamir Valley, an immense abyss of darkness. I don't look at the valley nor at my ultimate objective, Base Camp. I focus on the fifty metres below me that I can distinguish in the darkness. Time no longer exists.

I arrive at a belay, a junction point between two ropes. A stake or a screw is acting as an anchor, with several ropes connected, entangled. I have to work out what is safe and what can't be trusted at all. Then I stay connected to the rope above and I grab the lower rope in both hands. My left hand is above my right hand. I tug sharply on it to assess the echo returned to me by the rope. This way I know if I can slide on it for the duration of a descent, or whether I'll have to lighten the weight. The rope's solidity has been diminished by the passing seasons and by big temperature differences. Being made up of nylon fibres, the static ropes are not fit for climbing and are quickly frayed by the belay devices. After one season, I consider them to be dangerous. I bear in mind that they can break like glass.

I unclip myself from above. I wrap my leashes on the rope to form auto-blocking knots. A round turn on the fixed rope, which I connect to the screwgate karabiner on my harness's tie-in points. I apply tension to test the system. Two minutes' rest. I warm my hands, blowing on them. I close my eyes. I function by feeling. Then another forty metres of descent, climbing down the moonlit staircase.

> Normally, frostbite on the feet is excruciatingly painful. Typically, when the hands start to freeze, you lose sensitivity, and all handling of the rope, karabiner, etc. becomes difficult, even impossible after a certain time. Miraculously, I didn't suffer. I didn't have shooting pains in my foot; my hands suffered, but I managed to use them. Incredible luck, another miracle. Without sensation in my hands, any attempt to descend would have been in vain.

I keep expecting to get stuck at the end of a rope caught in the ice and to have to wait until daybreak to work out my next move. And yet, providentially, none of this happens.

Only five metres of rope are trapped in the ice. I must downclimb carefully, my hands placed on the black ice and the front points of my crampons firmly anchored for each step. Some ends are caught for one or two metres, but I can free them quickly with hard pulls on the rope. Each grab at the rope shoots pain through my fingers, but this is nothing compared to the suffering Tom endured from the summit to the crevasse, and still endures.

An insidious fatigue engulfs me. I try to breathe deeply to chase these emotions away. My mind detaches from the suffering that creeps into my flesh and slyly penetrates my fingers. With my left hand, I try without success to remove my overmitten. Exasperated, I tear it off with my teeth, dislodging the covering in front of my mouth in the process. My thin glove liners underneath are covered with frost. Bending my fingers to close my hand around the rope is painful, but I don't care. My fight is elsewhere; at this point my hands are a minor distraction which shouldn't interfere with my thoughts. A minor distraction that I assess constantly, because my survival also depends on my hands. I try to warm them up regularly by blowing on them. I make a circle with my hand and put my mouth between my thumb and forefinger, my other fingers curling on the palm of my hand. And I blow warm air from my lungs to try to bring my fingers back to life. Snow vortices sweep the slope once again, filling the overmitten that hangs from my wrist with snow crystals. Pain torments my extremities. I feel as though the blood is slowly returning. The intensity of the burn is sometimes violent. Then I empty my mitt and repeat the operation with the other hand. The shooting pains are torturing me, but I have to keep moving and focus on getting down.

The wind is increasing. I'm on the edge of a ridge when a violent gust almost makes me lose my balance. Small icy needles slap the unprotected part of my face. I think back to the hours of hope and despair that I endured the previous night on the ledge of that distant crevasse. It already seems far away. I'm now descending towards light; I'm confident. I pray that I might get this wind-exposed ridge over and done with. My left overmitten has just flown away in a violent gust! Shit, I only have my frozen glove liner on this hand!

Camp 2 isn't far away. I know, thanks to a message that Ludo sent me around 11 a.m., that Daniele Nardi and Alex Txikon left a tent there behind a boulder in 2016. I cling on to this idea; I am exhausted, but I will be able to shelter if I find it. Maybe there will be some food too. Maybe. It's a slim hope, but it motivates me.

Tomek and I had had a hard time on this descent once before, in 2015. We ran out of food and had nothing to drink. And even then, my only goal was Daniele Nardi's tent, as I knew that he'd left it at Camp 1. And we found it! We took shelter, I heated up some snow, and we were able to drink and set off again. The cook saw the light of our head torches and climbed up to meet us from Base Camp.

I fight; I suffer enormously with my fingers. The terrain is mixed, with ice, a lot of traverses, quite tricky. I have to grip the ropes as tightly as possible and the pain is intense: I feel like the ice crystals are solidifying in my fingers.

In retrospect, I condemn myself for the choice I made to descend alone. I could have stayed with Tomek, kept him company as best I could until his last breath. Then I could have come down. Or I could have waited for the heli with him.

When I returned home, the doctors assured me that Tomek had only a few hours to live when I left him. According to them, he was in the final stages of pulmonary oedema. Nothing could have saved him, not even a fast heli descent.

# 28 JANUARY 2018,
## 1.50 A.M.

Suddenly a beam of light from the slope below pierces the darkness.
A second follows twenty metres behind. Two beams that illuminate
a long way, moving quickly like agitated puppet heads. A mist blurs
the radiant yellow head torch. They climbed up? My God, they
climbed up, they climbed up!

I'm at the end of the rope, on a rock before the next section.
I shout out. But the sound is blocked; my vocal cords are obstructed
by the fierce frost of the night. I try again: 'Heeeeyyyyy! I'm here!'
A veil of comfort slides over me. Sitting on the rock, I watch the
ballet of light beams ascending towards me. The most fabulous
spectacle of my life.

They haven't heard me. My cries got lost, stifled by the snow and
carried on the wind towards Tomek. My heart thumps under my ribs,
striking up to my head.

I remain petrified, perched on my rock 100 metres above them.
Unable to move, to comprehend what is happening. It's 1.50 a.m. and
I'm at 5,950 metres, just above the usual Camp 2 of the route.

The lights arrive on the flat section. I continue to scream, in vain.
One of the climbers has taken the lead and is ascending alone.

Suddenly, twenty metres away, the beam of his head torch shines
on me and I hear: 'Adam, I have her!' It's Denis shouting! Denis
Urubko, my role model, my idol, the mountaineer who has always

impressed me, the man who inspires my immense respect but who I have never met before.

'Élisabeth, can you come down, can you join me, walk a little bit?'

'Of course, Denis.' Of course I can descend, but I'm so astonished by these unlikely events that I'm experiencing! All these hours of waiting, of hope, of despair. Ludo's last message pushed back a rescue effort to the following day. And yet they're here, at two in the morning!

I move, I descend, but already, suddenly, I've let go. My fingers hurt so much; the pain is so excruciating that I can no longer hold the karabiners. I feel clumsy. I take the rope and internally scream in pain. I try again, carefully, cautiously.

I join Denis. He hugs me. 'Élisabeth, Élisabeth, nice to meet you, Élisabeth. Adam, I have her! Adam, I have her!' His cries burst my eardrums, but I'm so relieved. They climbed up! I'm no longer alone; I'm with Denis!

I am happy. I know it's not the right word for this moment. Not appropriate, considering the situation. Tomek is up there. I see his face over and over, his hands, his voice, his gaze, his distress, his fear, his frustration. But I'm no longer alone with these thoughts, finally. For the first time, I can share them and talk about them with Adam and Denis. I feel supported, comforted, and I forget about my arduous pilgrimage to get here.

Denis shines his light on my hands and immediately gives me his mitts. He helps me to put them on, and he puts on my glove liners instead. 'But they're too cold – your gloves – they're frozen!' He quickly takes out another pair of gloves from his bag for himself.

'Don't use your hands any more,' he tells me. He attaches me to the rope and brings me down to Adam Bielecki.

Adam is a great friend. We met in December 2015 at Nanga Parbat Base Camp. We hit it off immediately. I've always had a lot of respect for him. We had planned to climb Everest together in 2016, to open a new route on the north side. But he broke his wrist on a slackline just beforehand.

'Oh, Éli, I am so glad I found you!' Adam wraps me in his arms. Immediately, he asks me: 'Can Tomek walk?'

'No, Adam, he can't.'

'Éli, I'm sorry, but we can't do anything. It would take six people and oxygen cylinders to get him down. I'm sorry, Éli.'

The words ricochet under my skull and a sense of anguish is etched into my cortex. I reason with myself: I understand that they can't ascend by helicopter now because of the weather conditions. But in my head, at this moment, the helis are going to take off the following day for Tomek. I'm worried about time ticking on and the intensifying gusts of wind, even though Tom is well protected in his crevasse, impervious to wind and snowfall.

How did I not understand at that time that Tomek was condemned? The reality was too difficult, too heavy to bear. My mind obscured and rejected the evidence, preferring to still envisage a possibility of helicopter rescue. Denis had already anticipated and made the decisions in advance, with Adam and the Polish support team. On his return, this is what he wrote:

'It was up to us to make a choice. We are not children. We are mountain professionals. We were very unlikely to find Tomek alive after all those hours spent up there, without food or water, especially given the state he was in. How, then, could two of us have transported him over the vast plateau at 7,200 metres, then down the face? If we'd had the slightest chance of saving Tomek, we would have gone, but we quickly realised there that we should focus on saving Élisabeth alone. Tomek was a warrior. He made the choice to be a fighter.'

And this is what Adam wrote:

'It was like a death sentence. I knew that even if we could climb 1,400 metres more, which was almost impossible, we wouldn't be able to do anything for him. We wouldn't be able to bring him down by carrying him if he couldn't walk.'

Adam hands me his Camelbak. I suck on it endlessly. He takes the tip from me. 'Éli, be careful; don't drink too quickly. You haven't drunk anything for a long time. You're going to puke.'

'I'm too thirsty, Adam. Thank you, thanks so much, Adam!'

Denis joins us. They briefly discuss the plan and then Adam takes his radio and speaks in Polish to Jarosław and Piotr, who stayed at Camp 1 to prepare a bivouac. Denis and Adam disagree about the next part – take a short break or descend straight away? They speak in English, contradicting each other like an old couple. The situation, because it's so human, makes me smile inside.

Adam wants to reach Camp 1 immediately in the dark because of the forecasted bad weather. Denis wants to wait until daybreak to tackle the Kinshofer wall. They talk, discuss it further, argue. Both of them need to sit down and drink too.

The wind comes in freezing gusts. Tiredness overwhelms me; I've been fighting terribly for the last few hours to not fall asleep. So I'm the one who cuts it short.

'I need a break. I'm out.'

Denis: 'Ah, Adam, here is a smart woman!'

They decide to organise a precarious bivouac, finding a level platform in black ice. They fashion together a tarpaulin and a sleeping mat. But the makeshift shelter flies in the wind. The mattress too. We have to hold everything down with crampons. And quickly pull everything over us.

Adam talks over the radio about the weather, Tomek's situation, his condition, the medication that I need to take. Finally, he helps me to take off my wedding ring, places it with his around his neck, and gives me some aspirin.

Denis melts ice with a small stove balanced on his knee. Side by side on the mat and under the shelter, we are in an extremely uncomfortable position for three people. My small size saves me, but they are folded in half! I tell them about the day of the 25th, the summit. I describe Tom's state to them. Then the wait, alone.

Adam tells me about their long wait at K2 Base Camp while the arrival of the helis was delayed: 'It was the most difficult moment of the rescue for me. I sent a photo yesterday morning to show the good weather from K2 Base Camp! I didn't know if we were going to fly or not, but it was obvious that if nothing happened today, a third night outside would have been fatal for you.'

We chat, eat, drink.

A few seconds later, all my energy leaves me; I'm wrung out. For the first time in hours, I can surrender.

I doze on and off. Adam, bent double, has extreme back pain. I keep drinking and talking about Tom, about our day on the 25th, the summit. It's immediately subject to questioning. Denis is habitually sceptical regarding performances, questioning summits, making terse judgements of the mountaineering domain. Adam too. GPS coordinates? No, I don't have them. Photo? No, I don't have that either. So, this will be a problem, they tell me. I don't care; I'm not claiming anything and I won't claim anything. 'But it's already on the internet, Éli!' they both warn me. What? How? I remember that I had indeed left a message for Ludo, I can't remember when exactly, but in a moment of great loneliness and distress. Why? Because I was alone, I needed to talk, needed Ludo to know that at least Tomek and I had managed to climb Nanga. But how did all this end up on the internet?!

I talk about our first night, about our hell, our slow descent into the night's apocalyptic temperatures. Adam tells me about the miracle that brought them here in so little time: 'I have tried three times in my life to get past the Kinshofer wall. Three times I failed! This night the wall opened up to us, thanks to the fixed ropes. After I had sworn never to pull on these ropes again! And yet it's thanks to them that we're here with you now.'

I doze lying across both of them. Denis holds me tight in his arms, wrapping me in warmth. The situation is unreal, strange, but this moment together has an intensity that I've never experienced before in my life.

Denis jokes: 'Éli, you have two gentlemen all to yourself; take advantage of it! We're lucky to have a woman like you with us!'

Meanwhile, Adam films us.

I still can't believe what's happening: in a few minutes, I went from hell to this cocoon of warmth. I drink. Adam gives me an energy gel, but I'm not hungry. Just thirsty, thirsty.

'You're a star now, Élisabeth!' Denis tells me.

'I'm the queen of frostbite, yes!'

In fact, at the time, I had absolutely no idea why Denis was telling me this. I was light years away from imagining the scale of media attention that the rescue had attracted. I was just emerging from the depths of hell and I was exhausted, dehydrated. The shift was stark. With Adam and Denis, I was relieved, happy; I knew that I had been saved. But I absolutely did not anticipate the 'madness' I was going to be sucked into upon my return, the condemnation and judgement from the mountaineering sphere or from strangers, the quest for the 'sensational', the relentless competition to wrest punchy words out of my distress. The factual, chronological account wasn't of interest; it needed tragedy. I wasn't ready for what hit me as soon as I arrived in Islamabad, then in Sallanches; I was unable to imagine the destructive spiral into which I was going to fall over the following months.

Time passes. I'm overtaken by fatigue. I doze in Adam's arms, then in Denis's. Adam has back pain; Denis mothers me, lies me on his legs, radiating as much heat to me as possible.

## 6 A.M.

Dawn arrives; it's almost 6 a.m. The shelter is being tormented by the wind – the gusts are incessant. Adam and Denis decide to descend, so they fold the shelter away. My hands hurt terribly. As soon as my fingertips touch something, the pain shoots straight up to my brain and I have to clench my teeth. But Denis reassures me: 'Your hands will be fine, don't worry; just avoid using them for now in order to protect them and prevent too much bruising by shocking the ice crystals in your flesh.' I also know that if I'm feeling pain, it's because I have circulation and the flesh is alive! My fingers have miraculously survived.

Denis and Adam organise the next part so that I don't need to grab the rope with my hands. Adam stays beside me; Denis gives me slack and lowers me. The abseil descent doesn't require any effort from me, neither physical nor psychological. I surrender myself in their arms. I act like a puppet; I just have to place my crampons to the best of my ability to stay balanced, and support my elbows against the wall to stabilise myself. I do what I can to help them without using my hands or hitting the wall. I feel like I've been transported on the glacier by the wave of a magic wand.

The start of the ridge is quite airy with sheer ice on some sections. The slope dives vertiginously on the right towards the Kinshofer wall and is lost in the still-dark depths of dawn. On the other side, cliffs obscure the view of the glacier some 1,000 metres below. I redouble my attention. The passage is dangerous. I think Adam is afraid I will lose my balance. After a few steps by my side, he's reassured; I walk well and with a sure step. He smiles: 'Great, Éli!' He attends to my every need. Just like Denis. Adam warns me that after the ridge, we will plunge into the slope to the right following the fixed ropes. I've been seeing and following them, these esteemed fixed ropes, for over twelve hours. Thank God for the Koreans who left them; they saved me from a tight spot.

Above, Denis has made a backup lowering system for us. I pay even more attention to the gusts of wind. I'm small in size, light and don't weigh very much against this staggering blast of air.

I grit my teeth every time my fingers make contact with the wall to rebalance me. But this is neither the time nor the place to express my suffering, so I say nothing. I have to control it. It's already truly incredible to be so relieved, helped by Adam and Denis. The ropes get tangled, criss-cross, overlap, fray; but they lead the way, as though the Archangel Gabriel had installed them for me, for us, and he has been blowing constantly on them since autumn to ensure that the snow wouldn't bury them nor the ice trap them.

We descend the Kinshofer wall. It's very steep but equipped: it's full of partially smashed ladders and the ends of old fixed ropes that have become tangled with more recent, but snapped, ones. It's a dump of nylon and metal here, but since yesterday I've been sliding along this jumble with a lot of gratitude.

I'm beside Adam; he's abseiling while Denis lowers me on the rope. I talk to Adam.

We arrive at the bottom of the wall. There's a big slope. I see that the route is fully equipped. A real miracle that enabled them to climb quickly, despite Adam having little confidence in the ropes. But today, all our safety protocols are flouted.

Adam starts to become exhausted, so he lowers me while Denis stays next to me. I'm thinking solely of reaching the sunny part below. I am really cold, frozen.

We do a few more abseils to overcome the sections of blue ice. Having reached the snow, I can descend facing out. To begin with, Denis puts himself in front of me to protect me. Adam is behind us. The lure of the sun, of Base Camp, drives me forward; I'm almost running. Denis is amazed! I allow myself to race towards life. My feet function by themselves; they want to flee, run away from this terribly cold shadow, escape from Nanga. I run towards the camp. I am happy to regain some speed, my sure steps, my nimbleness, the feeling of flying, carried by the sun and the radiance of life. Whatever test Nanga might deign to throw at me still, the prospect of getting off it overwhelms me.

We arrive at the bivouac set up in the night under Camp 1 by Piotr and Jarosław, two other members of the K2 expedition. They have already taken the tent down and descended to Base Camp by helicopter. Here, only our bags of equipment remain. We are grateful to find the sun. We take a break, recover the stuff. Adam takes a group selfie of the three of us. I take off my gloves. I'd like to send a message to Jean-Christophe, to Ludo, but the heli arrives.

The pilots of the very powerful Écureuil AS350 B3 helicopters have worked miracles since yesterday. They managed to drop the four climbers higher than originally planned. And that's probably what made the rescue possible: Adam and Denis had less distance to climb. Thanks to the fixed ropes, they were able to go faster, which was crucial as the bad weather was approaching.

## IN THE HELICOPTER

I stare at Nanga. I can't take my eyes off it; my gaze is magnetised to the place where Tom remains. I understand that I'm no longer physically present on the mountain, that my body is leaving its flanks. But my head, my thoughts, my emotions, everything is still up there. I wish, I pray that Tom might be strong, fight, battle. I hope he's warm, in the shelter of the hole. The noise of the rotor and blades of the helicopter, a sound as oppressive and heavy as my regrets, pulls me out of my thoughts. A black, oily sea seeps into me: the terrifying ink of darkness. I'm alive, but Tom is still in hell. I am eaten away by the idea of being alone here. And relieved at the same time. These two thoughts collide.

We land at Base Camp, where we find Piotr and Jarosław and load the rest of our belongings. There is a huge hubbub. I stay in the helicopter with the door open. Ghani arrives and says to me: 'Tomek missed the mountain, Tomek missed the mountain!' I melt in tears; all the last images of Tom come back to me. I fall to pieces.

I got out of this hell, but Tom is in a terrible situation. I feel terribly alone without him, torn apart. Despair seeps into me. I can't do anything. Nothing left, I can only suffer, continue to suffer …

From here, Nanga suddenly seems so hostile to me! It exudes a cold, sharp atmosphere, which chokes me. It is far removed from the wonderful place that Tomek and I travelled across when we were full of hope, joy and dreams, in a past that seems so distant.

The heli leaves for the Jaglot military base to refuel. The second heli, with Denis and Adam, joins us. I thank them, hug them. Any normal and pragmatic person would have abandoned us to our fate. Nobody was obliged to come to our aid. And yet Denis and Adam left their expedition on K2 and climbed up to find us and bring us help.

Adam gives me iloprost – a powerful vasodilator and anti-ischaemic – for my frostbite, to be used quickly in a drip to save my extremities. They have everything, these Poles! And I owe them everything.

I thank Denis for coming up, for coming to look for me, for saving me from this tight spot. 'You would have descended to Base Camp in any case, without us, I know it,' he replies. This man has a humility that moves me. Between Adam, Denis and me, there is now and forever a unique, unwavering bond.

Reuniting with my loved ones after this ordeal will be a shock. I can't write a message to Jean-Christophe without bursting into tears. I know where I've come from, but not where I'm going; the next part is going to be hard. I'm empty, broken …

The French ambassador to Pakistan arrives with the consul. Speaking in French feels good.

Finally, Jean-Christophe is on the phone, and his voice overwhelms me with emotion.

# THE RETURN

My return was hell. When I arrived in Islamabad, I was disconnected, 10,000 leagues from imagining the reach of our story, the final judgements that were already condemning me to burn in hell or setting me up as a heroine, the sensationalist headlines, the interpretations and inventions from all and sundry.

On the phone, Ludovic and the emergency doctor from Chamonix, Emmanuel Cauchy, spoke to me about this, but I could neither imagine nor understand that our rescue was making the headlines on television news. Even when my father, on the phone from the Drôme, told me this, it didn't hit me. I couldn't comprehend it; my head was elsewhere.

Afterwards, I was lost for a long time, still on the flanks of Nanga, fighting alone on the mountain, in the dark, without Tomek. Alone in this hell, internally cut off from the world around me. Even if I tried to put a brave face on it, my body and all my being remained clinging to Tomek and Nanga in a world inaccessible to anyone other than me.

I couldn't live with the irreparable. The adversity on Nanga had been too intense. The truth broke my heart. I was withdrawn, with a stony face and glazed eyes. A dull pain gnawed at me, annihilated me. Up there, Tomek had remained caught in the trap, and I had spent days and days, even after my return to France, trying to understand the incomprehensible. In Islamabad, and again on my arrival in

Sallanches, my mind still couldn't grasp that the rescue effort couldn't do anything, that no helicopter would go up and look for him. My brain refused to accept that Tomek had stopped living!

I couldn't do anything any more. I was no longer able to change anything, but I didn't face up to this. I couldn't have saved him; the descent had been tragic. I was mad at myself, I felt guilty, I hurt from much pain deep inside me. My heart was raw, bleeding. Often, tears flowed down my face without my even realising it, without being able to control them. Tomek's voice, his eyes, the appalling image of his frozen face, his fists forever closed and locked tight by the cold, haunted my days and my nights. I had, however, done all I could to save him, to snatch him from this terrible fate.

But he was dead and I was alive. And even this life was a nagging torture. I was drowning in the bottomless depths of remorse, of guilt. I was torn apart. The suffering caused by the frostbite on my toes and hands remained trivial compared to what I felt: a pierced heart, a wounded heart, a heart smashed to pieces. I was almost happy to suffer physically, in order to experience a little of what Tomek had endured in martyrdom.

I no longer recognised myself. I constantly had a knotted throat, and tears gushed all the time. I couldn't shake an unbearable feeling of emptiness, and the guilt wouldn't leave me. Maybe it never will. The self-reproach will always be there. I will have to learn to live with it.

I was gradually realising that I could have stayed up there, to wait for rescue or the end. I had escaped from this fatal delay, which would inevitably have resulted in the loss of Tomek and maybe of me. The doctors kept telling me that Tomek had certainly died shortly after I left. What would I have done if I had stayed with him, wiped out by despair? I might have slid into nothingness. Or would I have forced myself to fight, to get down, carrying with me the awful vision of Tomek's deserted body?

I will never know. There were no good options remaining. After our arrival at the summit, it was too late. But I was plagued by guilt, lambasted by futile and devastating remorse, with questions that just kept resurfacing.

Since January's miraculous rescue, our story had caused a lot of ink to flow, and all these words about what we had done and lived through up there caused new suffering, hurling me into a new abyss where the judgements and comments were like stones thrown at us. Only Tomek and I experienced the heartbreaking, dramatic story intimately.

However, there was also a lot of solidarity and kindness that accompanied and enabled my return – new friendships were born. But I was destroyed by the negative thoughts, the hasty judgements, the insults; until I got help and was encouraged to see something other than guilt, to leave the past behind, stop worrying about the future and try to live in the present. I was torn between the tragedy I was still living and the outstretched hands of my loved ones trying to stop me falling apart again.

I went through what is commonly called 'stages of grief'. First came anger directed at everyone: starting with me, of course, but also Ludo, Pakistani aid, Ali (our agent), and even Tomek. I was full of compassion for him, but at the same time so angry with him for having violated the safety measures that we had established together: always stay in tune with your body, keep something in reserve, don't put yourself in danger, don't take risks other than those inherent to the high mountains, warn the other person, manage the descent carefully.

I was hugely annoyed with him, because you shouldn't just go to pieces like that up there when you are experienced! He was so strong, my Tom – a real tractor, super tough. We had always rigorously studied the risks during our expeditions in order to minimise them as much as possible. But this time, Tom had overlooked some warning signs, it's undeniable. And I didn't know how to spot these signs; I didn't know to insist on turning back.

We are both responsible for this drama and the cascade of small mistakes which led to disaster. I am responsible for not being able to bring Tomek down, and Tomek is responsible for not being able to give up or go back down. But only Tomek paid the high price, and I alone am alive today.

During a press conference in Chamonix on 7 February 2018, the day I left hospital, our story became public, sped around the world, and elicited no end of comments on the television, on the radio, on social networks, in the newspapers, etc. It was hell for me. What I had experienced on the mountain was nothing compared to the violence of my return.

In the year that followed, even when I thought I was better and was trying to regain a social, professional and sporting life, the smallest thing was enough to push me back down into the depths of 25–27 January 2018 for days on end.

I realise today it was a miracle that we survived our first night outside after reaching the summit. A survival instinct caused my intuition and endurance to kick in so that I didn't collapse in the face of the dramatic situation we were living through.

I am still terrorised by the memory of the second night I spent alone in the crevasse. Surviving it was an even greater miracle: objectively, I should have been sliding little by little into lethargy from the cold, falling asleep forever, frozen in the crevasse. And yet I fought, with energy from an unknown source, to stay clinging to the world of the living.

On the third night, I walked with a calmness and a serenity which were intensified by the hopeless situation I found myself in, the feeling that I was hanging on by only a thread. The bright moon showed the way, lit up the fixed ropes. I was immersed in action, not in analysis. I moved forward, motivated by the hope of arriving at Base Camp and being able to do something to help the rescue team who would come to look for Tomek. I was relying on the ingrained skills acquired over my years of learning in the mountains, and they saved me that night. Until I met Denis and Adam. A miracle within a miracle!

The weeks and then the months passed. I started running again, cycling, climbing, going back to the mountains. Jean-Christophe and I went walking for a month and a half last winter in Mustang, and then in the Khumbu. I took the opportunity to return and solo some of the classic 6,000-metre peaks of the valley. Bit by bit, I rediscovered sleep, and the nightmares became less frequent.

But whenever I go cycling or running, the questions still swirl in my head.

What is my quest? What does it mean? And is it not a kind of voluntary imprisonment? I've realised that I always need projects in my life, and for me it's always about mountains and high summits. But need means addiction. I spend my time gilding the chains which hold me hostage to my need for altitude and escape. I'm not *addicted* to work, nor to television or food or prohibited substances, nor am I addicted to Facebook or Instagram. But I have been, and remain, addicted to high altitude and to Nanga.

Like Tomek, who in my eyes embodied freedom, non-conformism and independence. This was certainly one aspect of his life in the high mountains. But the other was addiction. And it's the same for me.

And then there's my perpetual and intimate dilemma where I remain divided between inclinations: on the one hand, I dream of being professional; on the other, I can't stand media exposure. I don't like clowning around on stage like I did last autumn during the mountain film festivals, even though the contact with the audience was special and warm, making for a positive and calming experience.

In 2016, I took a leave of absence from national education for two years to live my life fully as a mountaineer. After twelve years of teaching in the same way, I had become less motivated and could no longer stand the routine of school life. I increasingly felt like I was wearing a mask, appearing as an extra in my own life instead of being the author or director. In contrast, my motivation was inexhaustible in open spaces, and I grew with each new adventure, successful or not. And, moreover, the relationships that I experienced in the mountains

– with Tomek, of course, and with other roped companions – were stronger than all the relationships I had known in my teaching career. I also loved seeing the smiles of kids from the other side of the world, and the moments of daily life captured on the banks of the Indus River mattered to me more than anything.

It was not a simple choice; it was a new way of life that would upset my everyday reality, the equilibrium with my husband. It was a jump into the unknown from a financial and professional point of view, to abandon the comfort of habit. But I finally listened to myself and prioritised what lit up my life. Nobody would decide for me any more.

I have never regretted this choice. It hasn't been easy; sacrifices had to be made. The magic is that as soon as it was set in motion, everything faded: the fears, the questions, the doubts which bored into my nights. I could concentrate on the present moment. The highest of climbs was happening inside me. Step by step, I climbed my interior mountains. So I spent three winters far away from my loved ones, in discomfort, cold but happy.

I understand that I also bear responsibility for trying to constantly surpass my achievements. Ever harder challenges, a need to feel like I'm living in severe, hostile conditions. A need to push my body as far as possible. A need to challenge my psyche, my mindset and my motivation.

I like the comfort of my daily life in the Drôme. I'm happy there, and I need all the things that make life easy, pleasant and sweet. But I get bored quickly. And soon, the fear of 'fading away', of taking too much care of myself, of letting myself get sucked into the artificiality of social and professional life, returns. Very quickly, the vertigo of stillness sweeps over me: the worry of wasting my time, the fear of no longer feeling the intense emotions that I experienced up there, the bliss and serenity that I attain thanks to maximum physical exertion, commitment and confrontation with environments where I am almost alone in the world.

I don't go up there to fight – I hate warrior analogies for mountaineering, like the dramatic stories of mountaineers in distress. I go up there to live life fully, my life.

But how do I find the balance between passion and reason? Too strong a passion imprisons; a reason that is too rigid causes a loss of momentum, of freedom. How do I stop myself being overtaken by my own choices and prevent myself from being locked into my passion? How do I stop myself being carried away by ego, which in our society is based on evaluation, comparison, rivalry? How do I get back to my personal quest? Why, for example, did I choose to try this complicated route on Nanga Parbat in winter? Did I go off the rails? Did I pick the wrong objective? Did I go astray, far from my original path? From my initial desire, which primarily consisted of discovering the world from up there on the summit of the Earth? Do I deserve the label I've been given?

Maybe I was my own worst danger, my worst enemy sometimes. Too locked into my projects, advancing with blinkers fixed on my goals and those alone, tirelessly shaping my body, bending it over backwards without showing much respect for it. Eager to satisfy my desires above all, fearing eternal regret if I failed to fulfil my dreams; living in the past (what I did) and the future (what I want to do and where) but neglecting the here and now, the present: what am I going through right now; what are my feelings?

During this year of forced 'calling into question', I was obliged to learn to reconcile with my body. I experienced the desire and the need to detach myself from performance, to return to the primary objectives from which my ambition had diverted me, to rediscover authenticity – a new perspective on myself, on the world.

On the other hand, if I cut myself off from the high mountains, am I still me? They are an essential part of my life, and make me exist fully. Up there, I experience a one-on-one encounter which involves only the mountain and me. I go to the mountains, alone and of my own volition, for pleasure, without ever forgetting that we are only passing through here.

# 23 MAY 2019

A funny spring! There are many, many hopefuls for the summit of Everest at Base Camp, but there have been so few weather windows since the start of April that far too many candidates are leaving simultaneously today for the *push*.

I started late, around 10 p.m., whereas departure is usually at 7 p.m., to try to avoid the traffic. But I don't have a big margin, because the weather is due to turn at midday. Wind and snow. Leave later in the day, this has been my strategy from the start. It has worked well, allowing me to escape the tide during the climb from Base Camp.

But tonight, there's a blockage: I am slowed down for the first time at around 8,500 metres. An hour of waiting! No possibility of overtaking. The wind picks up, gusts of snow form, the cold is very sharp. It stings!

The same happens again a bit higher, just below the south summit at around 8,700 metres. I came with the idea of exploring a new unknown, experiencing an ascent beyond 8,500 metres without the assistance of supplementary oxygen, plumbing my depths in order to succeed in this challenge. I find that using oxygen is cheating at the game of altitude and placing the goal above the means. It also eliminates a part of my inner quest. But at this precise moment of ascent, on this particular day in my life as a Himalayan mountaineer, it seems like the 'oxygen or no oxygen?' dilemma doesn't really make sense any more, because on Everest, like on the world's other tallest mountains, you can't really talk about mountaineering or even performance any more. The fixed ropes cancel out any notion of climbing, with few decisions to be made and no autonomy, as well as nullifying every element of introspection on the route in the face of an adventure, an expedition. The ascent of Everest is now a reflection of our 'safe' society, of 'consumption': sanitised, with a good success/ speed ratio. Nowadays, adventure and exploration are to be found elsewhere. Everest has become commonplace. Here, we can't talk of climbers, but rather 'jumarers': you haul yourself up with the jumar handle more than you work your way up or climb. High-altitude porters install the camps, and often direct all the logistics. I have a deep respect for the Sherpa community, these forces of nature, working silently and tirelessly on the mountain. Caring for clients, they put everything in place to guarantee success.

And yet, in the days since my arrival at Base Camp at the start of April, I've noticed that each of the 'summit contenders' has a personal history with Everest, a singular, legitimate and respectable motivation; and they each live out their own adventure in the end, even under these sanitised conditions. My perspective on these candidates for the Roof of the World has evolved, changed. I now understand: they too are looking for a parenthesis in their daily lives, a 'lighter' life, weightlessness, for a few weeks.

As far as I'm concerned, I have only one leitmotif this spring: to take no risks, to reclaim my life in the environment that has been mine for so many years, to escape in the romanticism of these mountains that I love, to tread the object of my childhood dreams by the points of my crampons.

But my initial plans are shaken up: an ascent without oxygen won't tolerate stopping for an hour; the climb must stay fluid. Otherwise, the cold immediately grabs you and it becomes dangerous to remain stationary for a long time at these extreme altitudes. I am very well acclimatised: I even went up to 8,400 metres a few days ago, on the slopes of Lhotse. But despite this preparation, today there is only one alternative in the face of the 'traffic jams', the slowdowns: either I give up and go back down, a complicated option because there will also be a lot of people going in this direction; or I play it safe and take some oxygen as a backup. Do I want to stay true to the ambition that has driven me since I became a mountaineer? To my mountain philosophy? To my image? Or do I give priority to my feelings, to my childhood dream, to the goal that I'm pursuing today, a year after my return from Nanga? These icy features, glistening in the sun or severe in the cold shade, are the sentinels I've been seeking forever. I decide, choosing to use oxygen to enable me to reach the summit.

Essentially, I'm only here this spring to fulfil this dream, to get away from my life as an athlete, my quest to go ever higher and further, and to close this important chapter of my life. This year, I've dropped any vague desire for performance. I've ignored the labels I've been branded with. I've paid no attention to what others are doing – those who have inspired me, those I admire. I just want to reconnect with myself, repair and reclaim a part of my life; to finally tread on the Roof of the World, set foot on all these routes that I imagined and visualised, and stir up my emotions on this mythical mountain. What a joy it is to be here today! Rediscovering myself on Everest, after all that I experienced on Nanga and ever since my return, means much more than climbing on the Roof of the World; it's an inner Everest, the poetic, enigmatic, even dramatic, ascent of my life.

Each step is heavy in this second part of the ascent. I need to dig deep inside myself, in my guts, to find the energy to move forward. At altitude, I always discover an inexhaustible source of energy from within, an indefinable force.

Over the course of my steps, I feel the person I really am being reborn in me, the person with whom I've had no contact these last months. I finally find myself in this intensity of exertion and concentration. The altitude is working its magic. I allow myself to be absorbed by the ambiance of the mountain, by the elements, the cold, the frost, the void, the slopes, the night, the effort, the moon, the stars. I get lost in it all.

I am fulfilled, blissful.

The profile of the route is magnificent. I pick out the summit in the distance above a huge meringue of snow. What energy it exudes! An airy route, tapered, with the Rongbuk glacier on one side and the Khumbu on the other. Wow! I have rarely walked on such a beautiful ridge. I don't know if my view is rose-tinted, or if it's this beauty, after so many years of dreaming about it, which touches me deep inside, but I am ecstatic.

On the last stretch, there are few people and the wind gets stronger. The Hillary Step. I think of the first ascensionists, the pioneers Tenzing and Hillary. Total respect. I advance from wonder to wonder, but also from page to page through the books of my childhood. What bliss! Everything reconnects, everything takes on meaning; it's magic. Chomolungma, 'goddess mother of the world' in Tibetan, is one of the wonders of our Earth! At the summit, finally, the view is exceptional. A whole part of my life vibrates here. Today, I am no longer just contemplating a poster in my room; I'm there: a successful conclusion at 8,848 metres! Everest remains a serious ascent, with or without oxygen.

I descend with a fire in my heart, ablaze with renewed energy!

Back to Camp 4 in the storm. I think of Lhotse; I want to go back there. I know it from having set foot there in May 2017, alone. I lived one of the most intense moments of my life there, savouring each metre in an exceptional moment of grace and solitude. To withstand the wind, I had to reach the summit hunkered down. I could only stay there for ten seconds, but they were ten seconds of extreme intensity. I had a feeling of freedom and lightness, as though the mountain was absorbing my whole being, as though I were at one with her. I had no more will or thought: a gift which nature alone can offer. The wind was howling and I was thrilled! On the descent to Base Camp, several Sherpas who even knew my first name congratulated me and wished me good luck on Everest. How did they know me? Maybe simply because a girl climbing alone on these summits, without oxygen or Sherpas, is rather unusual, if not to say very rare. I returned to France in June, very emaciated but satisfied, captivated by the land of thin air. I had flirted with my limits, I had enjoyed the luxury of escaping from routine, from habits, getting out of my comfort zone to live in a different rhythm, beyond the confines of time. I felt as though I was a little bit closer to heaven.

This spring, I have only walked on Lhotse's sides to acclimatise. But the desire to continue, to climb to the top, torments me. Will I be able to set off in a few hours? Will my body be sufficiently recovered to go back up? Will the bad weather calm down? While waiting, I hydrate, rest, contemplate.

10 p.m. Not possible.

Midnight. Still not possible.

# 24 MAY 2019

3 a.m. I can finally stick my nose outside. I prepare water, nibble a bit of food and rush from the south col to the summit of Lhotse. The window is short, I know; wind is forecast mid-morning. I only have a few hours. My legs respond and I'm hungry! Everything is fine. The night is magical and I'm alone to savour it. A very different moment from yesterday. I turn around: there are few head torches on Everest today, and nobody on Lhotse. The couloir is dry this year. A helmet is not a luxury item there.

The sunrise over Nepal and the Valley of Silence is magnificent. The view is my fuel for the day. What luck! I indulge myself in my kingdom, far away from the world, in my element, in solitude. In 'sensible robot' mode! The mountain welcomes me with kindness for the time being; there is no wind. I know these routes well and I can see the mixed summit section.

9.20 a.m. I'm on the summit of Lhotse once again! I'm alone and even the wind leaves me in peace. I savour the ocean of mountains around me. Tibet, Nepal, Everest, Makalu, Lhotse Shar, Base Camp in the distance. A gift. Such happiness accumulated in two days!

I finally feel like myself again. These last few years, I let myself get carried away by an image, perhaps by the race for achievement too. The road from Nanga has been long, and strewn with many intimate sufferings. But today I returned to my primary, inner quest. I found myself again: a spirit carried on the winds, a little dazed but happy.

Everest–Lhotse, my convalescence, my closure. A sensory ascent between two worlds. An existential quest. One step closer to my true self. On these peaks, among the winds and the Tibetan prayer flags, the oppression, despair and bitterness that had been eroding me have vanished into thin air. Life is today, in front of me.

# ABOUT ÉLISABETH REVOL

1979:       Born on 29 April in Crest (Drôme region, France).

1999:       Began climbing and mountaineering while studying STAPS (science and technique of physical and sporting activities).

2005:       French national team of young mountaineers in the FFCAM (Fédération Française des Clubs Alpins et de Montagne). First expeditions to faraway places.

2005–2015: Alternated between teaching PE at middle/high school level and travel/Himalayan mountaineering (on the highest mountains in the world, alpine style, without supplementary oxygen or porters, sometimes solo, sometimes in winter). Passion for winter conditions at very high altitudes.

### EXPERIENCE

2000–2010: Big routes in the Alps (north face of the Drus, north face of the Grandes Jorasses, Droites, Verte, Courtes, Eiger, Matterhorn, Ailefroide, Pelvoux, Meije, etc.).

2006:      First expedition to Bolivia, in the Illampu massif, with a team of young mountaineers. Established several mixed routes on the Pico Schultz, Aguja Yacuma and Illampu.

2007:      First ascent and traverse of Pharilapcha in Nepal.

2008:      First 8,000-metre peaks on the Baltoro glacier (normal routes, alpine style). Link-up of Gasherbrums I and II.

2009:      Annapurna East, new route in alpine style, south-east face, then a traverse from the east to the north.

2009–2013: Adventure racing competitions with Team Lafuma.

2013:      Nanga Parbat in winter, alpine style, via the Mummery Spur, up to 6,500 metres.

2014:      Alpinism/Biking trip to Tajikistan on the Pamir route and ascents of virgin peaks in Kyrgyzstan in the foothills of the Inylchek glacier.

2015:      Back to Nanga Parbat, alpine style again, but this time via a route ascending the Diama glacier. Altitude reached: 7,800 metres.

2016:      Nanga Parbat once again up to 7,500 metres.

2017:      Lhotse (normal route).

2017–2018: Nanga Parbat with Tomek Mackiewicz, new route in alpine style on the west/north-west face.

2019:      Everest–Lhotse (May); Manaslu (September).

## NANGA PARBAT ROUTES

### EISENDLE/MESSNER ROUTE
On the north-east face, on the Diama glacier, an attempt was made in July 2000 by Reinhold and Hubert Messner, Wolfgang Thomaseth and Hanspeter Eisendle.

### REVOL/MACKIEWICZ ROUTE
This route was repeated three winters in a row by Élisabeth Revol and Tomasz Mackiewicz: including up to 7,800 metres in 2015, then to the summit on 25 January 2018 by joining the exit of the normal route with a more direct traverse.

### KINSHOFER/NORMAL ROUTE
After an attempt the previous year, Siegfried Löw, Toni Kinshofer and Andreas Mannhardt opened the first route on this face in 1962. It was the second successful ascent after Hermann Buhl's in 1953.

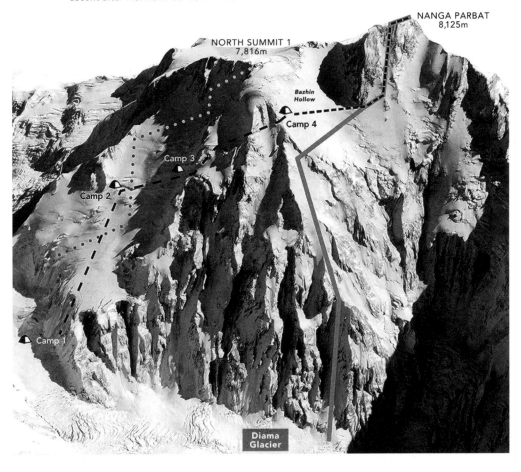

· · · · · · ·  Eisendle/Messner route
     July 2000

- - - - - -  Revol/Mackiewicz route
     January 2018
     To summit: 8,125m

————— Kinshofer/Normal route
     1962
     To summit: 8,125m

# RESCUE TIMELINE

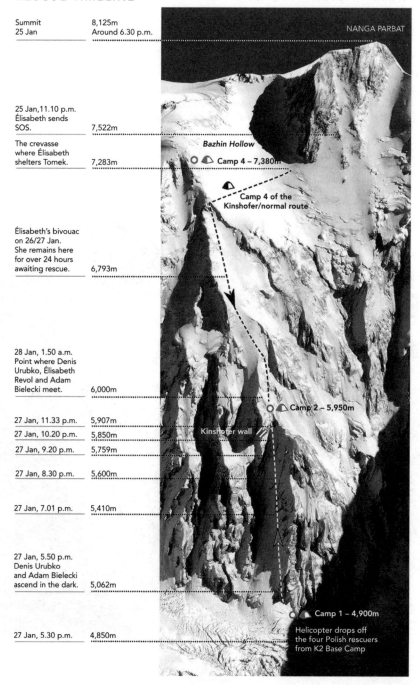

| | | |
|---|---|---|
| Summit<br>25 Jan | 8,125m<br>Around 6.30 p.m. | NANGA PARBAT |
| 25 Jan, 11.10 p.m.<br>Élisabeth sends<br>SOS. | 7,522m | *Bazhin Hollow* |
| The crevasse<br>where Élisabeth<br>shelters Tomek. | 7,283m | Camp 4 – 7,380m |
| | | Camp 4 of the<br>Kinshofer/normal route |
| Élisabeth's bivouac<br>on 26/27 Jan.<br>She remains here<br>for over 24 hours<br>awaiting rescue. | 6,793m | |
| 28 Jan, 1.50 a.m.<br>Point where Denis<br>Urubko, Élisabeth<br>Revol and Adam<br>Bielecki meet. | 6,000m | |
| 27 Jan, 11.33 p.m. | 5,907m | Camp 2 – 5,950m |
| 27 Jan, 10.20 p.m. | 5,850m | Kinshofer wall |
| 27 Jan, 9.20 p.m. | 5,759m | |
| 27 Jan, 8.30 p.m. | 5,600m | |
| 27 Jan, 7.01 p.m. | 5,410m | |
| 27 Jan, 5.50 p.m.<br>Denis Urubko<br>and Adam Bielecki<br>ascend in the dark. | 5,062m | |
| | | Camp 1 – 4,900m |
| 27 Jan, 5.30 p.m. | 4,850m | Helicopter drops off<br>the four Polish rescuers<br>from K2 Base Camp |

## HELICOPTER RESCUE MAP

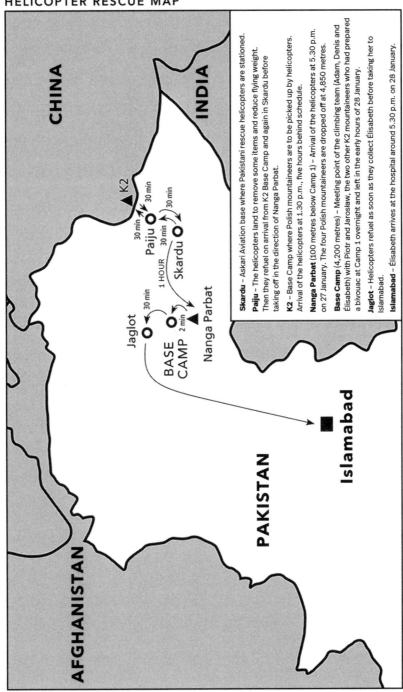

CHINA

INDIA

K2

30 min
Paiju O 30 min

30 min
Skardu O 30 min

1 HOUR

Jaglot
30 min O

BASE
CAMP O 2 min ▲

Nanga Parbat

■ Islamabad

PAKISTAN

AFGHANISTAN

**Skardu** – Askari Aviation base where Pakistani rescue helicopters are stationed.

**Paiju** – The helicopters land to remove some items and reduce flying weight. Then they refuel on arrival from K2 Base Camp and again in Skardu before taking off in the direction of Nanga Parbat.

**K2** – Base Camp where Polish mountaineers are to be picked up by helicopters. Arrival of the helicopters at 1.30 p.m., five hours behind schedule.

**Nanga Parbat** (100 metres below Camp 1) – Arrival of the helicopters at 5.30 p.m. on 27 January. The four Polish mountaineers are dropped off at 4,850 metres.

**Base Camp** (4,200 metres) – Meeting point of the climbing team (Adam, Denis and Élisabeth) with Piotr and Jarosław, the two other K2 mountaineers who had prepared a bivouac at Camp 1 overnight and left in the early hours of 28 January.

**Jaglot** – Helicopters refuel as soon as they collect Élisabeth before taking her to Islamabad.

**Islamabad** – Élisabeth arrives at the hospital around 5.30 p.m. on 28 January.

# LETTER TO TOMEK

Little by little, my memory comes alive, the gaps are completed and my emotions translate into words. The pages fill up and I move forward in the gradually dissipating fog. My mind remains attached to Tomek, to Nanga and to the emotions experienced up there with him, then without him. When I'm alone, thousands of words, nuances, come to mind simultaneously. Perhaps it's the power of words to relieve sorrows. I think only of him; I think about his life, his philosophy, his way of living, his love for Nanga …

Until now, it was impossible for me to write this letter.

Tomek was one of the freest and most independent men I know. He was out of the ordinary. The Himalayan mountaineering he practised on Nanga in winter was his way of life …

Ten years ago, he was looking for opportunities; he wanted to live his adventures, those which would allow him to realise his dreams, those that would make him come alive.

He decided to face the unknown with Marek, guided by the certainty that it is by climbing, by exploring, by forging ahead that we live!

Tomek had freely decided to be free, to make the purity of the mountains his noble passion. He faced the heady extremes of climate, of nature.

Today I'm writing you a farewell letter, but I prefer not to end it by saying goodbye to you, because this is still impossible for me.

I lived unique moments with you; I felt extraordinary things and we did beautiful and authentic things together.

You will continue to be a part of me in many ways, because when we discover people like you and let them into our mountaineering life, it's impossible to erase the traces that they leave behind.

Your smile will forever be etched in my heart and the sparkle in your eyes will light up my days.

Every time you spoke, I saw the magic shine in the eyes of those who listened.

You were a great man, a monument, a myth, a genius of Nanga in winter, an agent of energy and desire. Of dreams and of life.

Tomek is one of the people who gave me the desire to spend time on this mountain, to soak up its silence, to dare to take this step towards the unknown, this step towards self-discovery, this step towards discovering its possibilities. It was with you up there that I understood what you could feel, what pushed you to always go further and spend so much time up there. This sense of vastness that does not overwhelm us, but instead gives us the desire to fly up towards the peaks, the heavens, space, dizziness. The power of the Universe, as you put it …

I don't know when you crossed the threshold. If only I could have noticed this sign! I don't know when I started losing you, when you passed the point of no return, if you yourself felt it.

Ninety metres below the summit, you were still fine. After that, we spoke little, but no less or no more than before. We always climbed in this way, concentrated. I still don't know how everything led to saying farewell today. The only thing I sense is your absence, and a whole wave of feelings.

We climbed this difficult winter route together, because we built our story on our true emotions, this fundamental life experience …

You were a man with a big heart and you fought up to the end to descend as low as possible in order to save my life. I owe my life to you in the first place, Tomek, because if you hadn't had the strength and courage to fight to descend to 7,280 metres, in survival mode, during the freezing, inhumane night of 25–26 January, I would no longer be here, but I would be with you …

We both knew there was no room for error; we accepted this. If one of us crossed their limit, the other would fall in turn …

Meeting a person like you remains rare, exceptional. You were the gentleman of Nanga and you were on this mountain once more to have no regrets, to complete your project and simply to live.

Tomek, you had an infinite passion for this mountain, a look in your eye bursting with energy for Nanga. You had the vigour and the strength to live your dream and see it through to the end.

Nanga was your inspiration, your writing and the book of your life.

On Nanga, our roped team was born: a happy team, a unique bond, with the same mindset.

Tomek, you passed through my life like a breath of air that infused me with the energy of *your* mountain.

You gave me this great and beautiful energy that I carry with me today.

Tomek, beyond Nanga, meeting you will remain an exceptional and unforgettable experience for me. A meeting of similar minds for dreams and adventures, a friendship based on simplicity, a crossing of paths that will forever retain the bittersweet taste of freedom.

Thank you, Tomek, for being what you were.

Élisabeth Revol, May 2018

# TRIBUTE TO TOMEK MACKIEWICZ

The Commander in Chief of Aviation in the Pakistani Army, General Khalil Dar, concluded his mission report on the rescue operation carried out on Nanga Parbat with these words:

> What a heroic end for one of the great mountaineers of alpine style, Tomasz Mackiewicz […]. Before leaving our world he could be proud of leaving his three children a legacy of being the first, with Revol, to climb a new route in winter and in alpine style on Nanga Parbat.[100]

Polish mountaineer Voytek Kurtyka, pioneer of alpine style in the Himalaya, with many first ascents of high mountains to his name, was a big inspiration for Tomek Mackiewicz. In Mariusz Sepioło's book *Nanga Dream*, which is devoted to Tomasz Mackiewicz, Voytek says of Tomek:

> I felt close to him because he set himself a challenge that went beyond 'common' Himalayan mountaineering in an extraordinary way. Tomek was the total negation of cut-price Himalayan mountaineering. Today, it's not about the challenge; this has been replaced by a commercial objective which attracts media attention and makes the climber a star, a celebrity. […] In an interview, Simone Moro explained with incredible honesty that he threw himself into

Himalayan mountaineering because it was the only chance to no longer be second after Messner. Tomek thought outside of this logic.

[...] Tomek had a strong compulsion which pushed him seven times on to the same mountain. [...] He knew that the crazy world of all 'the firsts', 'the best', 'the strongest' would not reward second place so generously. And yet, he returned.

[...] Mackiewicz made several fascinating solo attempts to summit Nanga in winter. He reached fairly high altitudes, but was unable to reach the top due to difficult weather conditions. [...] During one of these attempts, he spent a week at around 7,000 metres. He settled in snow holes and the mountain became his home. He did something incredible; he had a striking intimacy with the mountain [...]! I really envied him (in the best sense of the term). There is no greater satisfaction for a climber than to win the friendship of the mountain.[101]

# ADAM BIELECKI AND DENIS URUBKO, ICE 'GLADIATORS'

———————

In January 2018, two stars of Himalayan winter mountaineering, Polish climber Adam Bielecki, then thirty-six years old, and the Kazakh-Russian-Pole Denis Urubko, forty-five, were attempting a first winter ascent of K2, the second-highest peak in the world, on a Polish national expedition. They halted their ascent to rescue Élisabeth Revol and Tomek Mackiewicz. Alongside two other members of the expedition – Jarosław Botor, a nurse, professional rescuer and mountaineer; and Piotr Tomala, a rope-access contractor – they were helicoptered by the Pakistani Army to Nanga Parbat, where they rescued Élisabeth Revol and then returned to K2.

Denis Urubko, a former soldier from the time of the Soviet Union, had already climbed the fourteen 8,000-metre peaks without oxygen nineteen times, including two in winter (Gasherbrum II and Makalu), and had participated in several rescues in the Himalaya.

In an interview given on 28 January 2018 to the Spanish specialist magazine *Desnivel*, he stated:

> What was clear was that we could not cross our arms and wait. [...] I think any mountaineer in a similar situation would do the same as Adam and me. We had a lot of luck: we were able to use the helicopter, we were acclimatised, there was a budget to carry out

the rescue, we had the necessary equipment ... Doing our best was enough. We had to do it.

Tomek's rescue was impossible. We had to make a decision [...] the forecast was very bad for the next few days. We were not in a position to take on Tomek's rescue [...]

Of course, we are not completely satisfied, because we were unable to help Tomek. But it was great to be able to help Élisabeth Revol.

The Kinshofer route was equipped with fixed ropes installed by commercial expeditions. We found a lot of fixed ropes in good condition, which allowed us to ascend so quickly, without additional risk.

When we met Élisabeth, she was totally destroyed and her fingers were all white. She was frozen, very cold and very tired, but she is a very strong woman who accomplished something extraordinary. She descended alone, in a really extreme situation. She managed to descend slowly until we met. We spent a few hours resting in a small bivouac tent for two people (there were three of us). We gave her water and medicine and she was able to sleep a little, sometimes leaning on me, sometimes on Adam. We were happy to be able to help this great lady and mountaineer. Adam and I did not sleep at all. The important thing was that Élisabeth slept for a few hours.

She is a very strong woman. A woman who will be able to do great things in the future because she is a true mountaineer.[102]

# CROWDFUNDING

In total, crowdfunding made it possible to collect 157,000 euros, 80 per cent of which was sent by the Polish diaspora. The French government's advance of 31,000 euros for the rescue was able to be partially reimbursed by Élisabeth Revol's FFME global insurance (20,000 euros) and the rest through crowdfunding. The Polish government paid Tomek's share of the rescue. Each of Tomek's children received 44,000 euros thanks to the online collection. The remaining amount was allocated as shown in the diagram below.

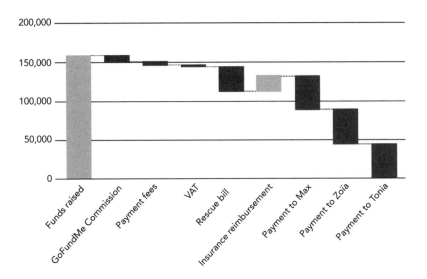

# ACKNOWLEDGEMENTS

I would particularly like to thank:

Jean-Christophe Revol for his eternal and absolute support.

I know what I owe to the Polish mountaineers who abandoned their ascent of K2 to try to save other mountaineers. An act of solidarity and exceptional bravery. Denis Urubko, Adam Bielecki, Piotr Tomala, Jarosław Botor and Krzysztof Wielicki: you are my life.

Thanks to Ludovic Giambiasi, 'my route-planner' from the start of the rescue, but also my connection with the mountain. He was able to find the right words to save my life.

Thank you to my parents, who opened my eyes to the mountains. To my brother, my most faithful training companion.

My infinite gratitude to Tomek Mackiewicz, and all my respect for his mystical fascination with Nanga Parbat (Fairy's call!), difficult for the uninitiated to understand, but who inspired each new attempt on this summit in winter.

Thanks to Anna Antonina Solska, Tomek's wife, and all my thoughts go to Tomek's three children.

Thanks to Daniele Nardi, a Himalayan mountaineer who knew both Nanga Parbat in winter and Pakistan perfectly, who became fully involved with Ludovic Giambiasi to better organise the rescue, and who disappeared in March 2019 on this mountain.

Thanks to Zbigniew Wyszomirski, consul of Poland in Pakistan.

Thanks to Michel Nehmé, consul of France in Pakistan.

Thanks to all the rescue team, who did a titanic job for over seventy-two hours, and particularly Agostino Da Polenza, Stefania Mondini and Maurizio Gallo.

Thanks to Dr Robert Szymczak, Janusz Mayer and the entire Polish K2 team, the alpine community in Poland and the Polish diaspora.

Thanks to Riaz Ul Hassan in connection with Askari Aviation, Brigadier Arkram Khan and General Khan at the head of Pakistani rescue efforts.

Thanks to Emmanuel Cauchy, the doctor who managed live telemedicine from Chamonix with Robert Szymczak.

Thanks to Yan Giezendanner, a meteorologist based in Chamonix, who provided detailed weather reports during the entire rescue operation.

Thanks to the Polish government, who did not hesitate to make a financial contribution to the rescue operation.

Thanks to the French Embassy in Pakistan, who spared no effort to resolve difficult situations.

Thanks to the Embassy of Pakistan in France for the many letters of support since my return and the important bond that unites us today.

Thanks to the helicopter pilots, who managed the complicated weather conditions as best they could in winter on Nanga Parbat.

In Pakistan where I met men with values, beliefs ... thank you. Thanks to the porters who carried our equipment to Base Camp; to Ghani, Tomek's friend in the Diamir valley.

Thanks to everyone who supported me with their messages, in any form; you perhaps don't realise how restorative and essential this has been for me.

Thanks to the SOS Gelures (frostbite) team (Hôpitaux du Pays du Mont-Blanc in Sallanches and the university hospitals in Geneva) and to Dr Frédéric Champly, as well as the medical teams who were able to find the right words and redoubled their kindness to make me forget my worries, in both France and Pakistan.

The collective generosity that manifested itself through the crowd-funding campaign warmed my heart; I think about all of these strangers who expressed their support and sympathy.

Thanks to the ingenious, pragmatic and proactive Masha Gordon, who was behind this campaign.

Thank you to all who supported me during the rescue operation and on my return. I can't name everyone but I will not forget anyone.

Thanks to Catherine Destivelle for the moral support, involvement in numerous media requests and help.

Thanks to Laetitia Briand and Anne Gery, who managed the media influx when I returned and helped us to deal with journalists.

Thanks to Éliane Patriarca and Valérie Dumeige, without whom this book would not exist.

# NOTES

––––––––––

The content of the inReach messages is reproduced verbatim in the notes, with the original spelling and punctuation.

1    Tomek: Tomasz Mackiewicz

2    *Oui ca va la form on tente quelque chose today si meteo ok sinon on redescend.*

3    Rare are the mountaineers who attempt an ascent of an 8,000-metre peak, even more so in winter, in alpine style, the most stripped-down style that exists: without oxygen, without fixed ropes, without assistance, without porters. Without any safety net.

4    To climb a face, we follow its 'lines of weakness', meaning the points where the slope is less severe, or the terrain less dangerous, thus enabling us to control the difficulty and to progress.

5    A Buff is a multifunctional accessory marketed by the Spanish company Original Buff SA: elasticated fabric in a tube shape, used as protection from the elements around the neck, as a face shield, to cover the nose or worn as a headband, hat, hood, etc.

6    The full message sent was as follows (sic): *Tomek need rescu soon frosbite and he didn't see nothing pleas manage something with ali sonner as you can. Tomek pas good besoin secours gelure et ne voit plus. Organise secours avec Ali aussi vite que possible. Altitude: 7 522m.*

7    *On organise ça prends pas de risque pour toi descends si nécessaire.*

8    *Merci c la merde ici je me gèle dehors et j'ai super peur pour Tomek.*

9    *Suis au tel avec Ali. Il essaie d'organiser ça. certain à 100 % dispo demain matin.*

10   *Peux-tu descendre seule ? On essaie de voir d'autres secours en plus d'Ali.*

11   *Je ne laisse pas Tom*

12   *seule pr moi ça craint vraiment gros glacier et tro loin tom*

13   *Tomek va survivre. Fais tout ce que tu peux pour lui mais j'ai confiance en lui, j'ai confiance en toi, en vous.*

14   *Hélico Ok entre 10 et 11 heures descends au max. On pense à toi. Love. Boire manger bouger.*

15   *On essaie secours terrestres en +. Ambassy. Army. Helico. You're not alone. Go down.*

16   *Climbers from k2 comes with 1 helico in case of. 2e hélico va vous récup où vous êtes. Share me position.*

17   *On essaie secours terrestres en +. Ambassy. Army. Helico.*

18   *Super je me pèle suis o bord crevasse limite a me faire gelure t'enverrais ma position GPS demain.*

19   *Descends au max*

20   *Es-tu à la tente? Situation toi tomek. Il faudra peut-être descendre un peu pour l'hélico.*

21   *Tomek est ds une situation terrible, ne peut pas marcher, on a pas pu rejoindre la tente ms fo l'évac au plus vite.*

22   *le vent se lève et Tomek saigne bcp de c gelures, infection ne va pas tarder. Altitude 7 273 m.*

23   On 26 February 2016, Simone Moro of Italy, Basque climber Alex Txikon and Ali Sadpara of Pakistan achieved the first winter ascent of Nanga Parbat by the Kinshofer route on the Diamir Face. The Italian Tamara Lunger, who took part in the final push, had to stop just below the summit, too weakened to continue.

24   *Ca traine pour l'hélico. On fait tout mais essaie de descendre au max. tiens bon.*

25   *Peux-tu descendre seule au maximum?*

26   *Si 7 200 équipe terrestre. Si dessous hélico.*

27 *on a débloqué 15 000 euros perso pour hélico mais pas encore parti.*

28 *Peux-tu passer par la Heisendle-Messner et descendre? Il faut remonter au col pour ça.*

29 *Si oui pars maintenant.*

30 *Tu dois descendre jusqu'à 6 000. Problème avec hélico.*

31 *non c'est la partie du glacier ki pu, sérac et big crevas et tro loin Tom.*

32 *par où veux tu descendre? On doit savoir pour organiser en function!*

33 *oui je peux descendre sur la voie Kinshofer, probablement 6 800. Dis moi juste quand?*

34 *Ok Kinshofer alors? Tu dois attendre 6 000 ... peut être 6 500 pour l'hélico.*

35 *6 800 possible avec hélitreuillage, garde baudrier.*

36 *OK descends où tu le sens. le plus bas possible. Mais indique nous pour helico.*

37 Translation of Polish text: *I love you very much, I will help you. Help is coming.*

38 *rescue team say: descend jusqu'à 6 000 m, on récup Tomek à 7 200 m et on te récup après.*

39 *envoie moi ta position et par quelle voie tu choisis de descendre. Idéalement 6 700 pour hélico.*

40 *Les hélicos se préparent. Soit pour aujourd'hui soit pour demain.*

41 *Tu es au top. Stay positive. On essaie envoyer un ce soir avec tente etc. Sinon demain 100%.*

42 *Je suis sans tente 3nuits rien dormi 24h ni bouffe, ni drink, Tom pire danger.*

43 *On fait tout notre possible. Tiens le coup encore un peu. te tiens au jus dés qu'il décident.*

44 *2 hélicos avec équipe, arrive prévue demain à 12h30. 13h15.*

45 *Monêtier en arrivant. On t'aime.*

46 *tu dois rester C3, il y a DZ.*

47 *Si tu decides autrement dis nous. Courage.*

48 *Tiens bon la nuit est longue mais finalement très courte par rapport à la vie qui t'attend.*

49 *Si tu lis ces mots force toi d'y répondre. Ne te laisse pas aller au froid. Tiens bon.*

50 *Urubko fait partie des secours. 6 personnes. 2 hélicos.*

51 IGN, the Institut Géographique National (now the Institut National de l'Information Géographique et Forestière), is the official reference for geographic and forest information in France. It specialises in aerial and ground surveys and mapmaking.

52 *donne des nouvelles stp les secours vont partir. Courage soeurette.*

53 Emmanuel Cauchy, emergency doctor and high mountain guide, specialist in cold conditions, founder of the Institut de formation et de recherche en medicine de montagne (Institute for training and research in mountain medicine, known as Ifremmont) in Chamonix. Also called 'Dr Vertical', he was swept to his death by an avalanche above Chamonix on 2 April 2018.

54 *Me suis gélée 5 orteils sur pied gauche ce du bois. foque je voi urgent Cauchy.*

55 *Tu as quoi avec toi?*

56 *Rien.*

57 *J'organise avec Cauchy. On est tous avec toi.*

58 *les secours sont en cours. tiens le coup.*

59 *les secours ont déjà récup équipe de secours au K2. Attend visibilité pour déco vers nanga.*

60 *baudrier sur toi? mousqueton double à vis? tout est prêt ils attende visibilité de leur côté*

61 *Mais la visibilité est bonne!!!*

62 *toujours en attente visibilité*

63 Yan Giezendanner, meteorologist and logistics planner in Chamonix.

64 *yan annonce fog a 15 mais nuit claire, donc ça devrait se dégager*

65 *on pousse pour qu'il décolle on ne maîtrise pas. Tu as du vent?*

66 *vent nickel ms plus bcp de tps avant nuage.*

67 *on pousse, on pousse, ils vont partir*

68 *on est dessus tiens bon sœurette. On te laisse pas on étudie tout.*

69 *les hélicos ont décollé, ils doivent faire un plein au milieu. On essaie encore un 3e hélico au cas où pour le relais*

70 *situation vent brouillard, tiens le coup*

71 *au cas où Alex a laisse bouffe à 6 000 m derrière l'arrête à droite down … dernier recours*

72 *encore deux heures avant l'arrivée des hélicos*

73 *2 h? ils partent d'Islamabad?*

74 *je pe essayer de descendre un peu! mais plus bien d'énergie*

75 *ce sommet arrivé de nuit nous coûte cher au final hormis notre bonheur*

76 *pour le moment rester sur possible zone atterrissage. Je te dis si tu dois descendre*

77 Jean-Christophe Lafaille was a French alpinist who was born in 1965 in Gap and died on 26 January 2006 on the slopes of Makalu, in Nepal.

78 *hélico pas très loin ca va comment?*

79 *ca va hyper soif et faim et dodo 5min*

80 *ils arrivent dans 30 mn. Rotation BC pour poser team. Et monter light.*

81 *Es-tu en possibilité d'attraper une corde en vol et bien tenir?*

82 *Avec des nœuds un corps mort? et mousqueton à clipper … prepare toi avec baudrier.*

83 *non ou avec mousqueton je suis bien cramée.*

84 *si ça fonctionne pas il essaie de se poser et sinon ils posent équipe.*

85 *Confirme nous. Secours ok? Si moindre problème dis moi on a un 3e hélico.*

86 *non pas secours*

87 *Tu ne les vois pas?*

88 *Non*

89 *Tu les entends? brouillard? ils sont sur place.*

90 *Person brouillard ok 3e hélico?*

91 *Je vais crever, bientôt plus de batterie.*

92 *new secours helico demain. scours team climbing. 6 000m tent bouffe ridge down right 10 min*

93 *J'essaie de descendre tant k'i y a des cordes.*

94 *rescue team say ne bouge pas.*

95 A French prusik is an autoblocking knot.

96 *Ma chérie, s'il te plait, sois au camp de base le 27!*

97    On 22 June 2013, during an abduction attempt which went wrong, ten foreign mountaineers and their guide were killed by an Islamist commando unit.

98    *Ma chérie, s'il te plaît, il faut que tu sois au camp de base le 27 janvier. Après, une grosse perturbation arrive. S'il te plaît, sois en bas le 27.*

99    The leashes are an elastic dual-strap system that attaches the ice axe to the tie-in points of the harness to avoid losing it, while allowing generous freedom of movement.

100    Extract from *The files of the GHM* (Groupe de Haute Montagne), 'One Thousand and One Nights on Nanga Parbat, final rescue', 27 April 2018.

101    Mariusz Sepioło, *Nanga Dream* (Znak Publishing, 2018). Translated from Polish to French by Kamila Wadecka.

102    Translated from Spanish to French by Élisabeth Revol.